C0-AQZ-994

COMPANIES AND MEN

Business Enterprise in America

This is a volume in the Arno Press collection

COMPANIES AND MEN
Business Enterprise in America

Advisory Editors
STUART BRUCHEY
VINCENT P. CAROSSO

*See last pages of this volume
for a complete list of titles*

THE ORIGIN AND DEVELOPMENT
OF A PHILOSOPHY
OF LONG-RANGE PLANNING
IN AMERICAN BUSINESS

David Ira Cleland

ARNO PRESS
A New York Times Company
1976

186790

658.4
C 6240

Editorial Supervision: ANDREA HICKS

———————◆———————

First publication in book form, Arno Press, 1976

Copyright © 1962, by David Ira Cleland

COMPANIES AND MEN: Business Enterprise in America
ISBN for complete set: 0-405-08062-X
See last pages of this volume for titles.

Manufactured in the United States of America

———————◆———————

Library of Congress Cataloging in Publication Data

Cleland, David I
    The origin and development of a philosophy of long-
range planning in American business.

    (Companies and men, business enterprise in America)
    Originally presented as the author's thesis, Ohio
State University, 1962.
    1. Industrial management--United States--History.
2. Planning--History. I. Title. II. Series.
III. Title: Long-range planning in American business.
HD70.U5C54 1976   658.4'00973   75-41751
ISBN 0-405-08068-9

THE ORIGIN AND DEVELOPMENT OF A PHILOSOPHY OF LONG-RANGE

PLANNING IN AMERICAN BUSINESS

ABSTRACT OF
DISSERTATION

Presented in Partial Fulfillment of the Requirements for
the Degree Doctor of Philosophy in the Graduate
School of The Ohio State University

By

David Ira Cleland, B. A., M. B. A.

******

The Ohio State University
1962

THE ORIGIN AND DEVELOPMENT OF A PHILOSOPHY OF LONG-RANGE
PLANNING IN AMERICAN BUSINESS

David Ira Cleland, Ph.D.

The Ohio State University, 1962

Recent attention given long-range planning in management literature stimulated research in tracing the origin and development of a philosophy of long-range planning in American business. Management literature was reviewed from contemporary periods back to 1885; military literature was reviewed for periods extending into antiquity. Primary research
was used to identify corporate practices, policies, and procedures with
respect to long-range planning. An extensive questionnaire was dispatched to 225 corporations representing a cross section of large American business. Ninety-one companies responded favorably to the query;
the questionnaire provided the main information for a reflection of the
contemporary aspects of long-range planning in American business.

Long-range planning, as an activity arising from the organic management function of planning, had its early development in the military
establishment. Concepts of long-range planning existed in business
circles before businessmen and scholars began writing about it; within
the military organization its origin can be traced back to antiquity.
Basic differentiation of long-range planning from short-term planning
centers around the time dimensions thereof and the internal and external
organizational considerations evaluated by the business organization.

During contemporary periods long-range planning became envisioned
as an intellectual process and encompassed a vast group of inter-relation-

ships of the elements of the business organization and its environment.
A high percentage of the large businesses surveyed are engaged in long-
range planning; long-range planning appears as a fairly well differentiated function of management. Specific procedures and techniques have
been developed for conducting long-range planning; future innovations
will be effected in long-range planning as the state of the art advances.

The existing philosophy of long-range planning is composed of a
framework of principles, ideas, and concepts which are given an identifiable separateness and unity of their own. Out of the thinking and writing of twentieth century practitioners and management literature has
arisen a body of belief and practices about long-range planning aimed
at achieving better business performance.

The contemporary philosophy of long-range planning did not develop
in a vacuum but rather evolved as the product of environmental factors,
forces, and effects. Long-range planning is predicated on certain premises and assumptions established from a comprehensive analysis and
evaluation of the internal and external environment in which the company
operated. Although contemporary thought had not developed a classic
definition of long-range planning, its philosophy pervades the organizational structure of a high percentage of the businesses surveyed and
thereby provides a framework from which general company activities are
conducted.

THE ORIGIN AND DEVELOPMENT OF A PHILOSOPHY OF

LONG-RANGE PLANNING IN AMERICAN BUSINESS

DISSERTATION

Presented in Partial Fulfillment of the Requirements for
the Degree Doctor of Philosophy in the Graduate
School of the Ohio State University

By

David Ira Cleland, B. A., M. B. A.

****

The Ohio State University
1962

Copyright by

David Ira Cleland

1962

ACKNOWLEDGMENTS

Throughout this study I have received very able support from many individuals. Their support has been a vital force which explains any contribution made by this dissertation.

I wish to thank the executives of the cooperating companies who provided answers to the extensive questionnaire used in the study. A special note of thanks goes to those executives who provided time for interviews.

I would like to acknowledge my appreciation to Professor Ralph C. Davis, Dr. Robert B. Miner, and Dr. William E. Schlender who served as my reading and examining committee and provided valuable counsel and assistance in developing the study.

Dr. Charles B. Hicks, my adviser during my studies at The Ohio State University, and also my counsel during the writing of this dissertation, deserves a special vote of thanks. He permitted me to grope through phases of research to discover for myself what I am sure he already anticipated. His optimism helped me over many hurdles.

My wife, Velma, is to be commended for her understanding and assistance. In addition to managing three lively children and a household she found time to type, tabulate data, and proofread the dissertation.

Finally, my heartfelt thanks to David, Jennifer, and Matthew for enduring my long absences from home. I hope this dissertation, and what it represents, is a partial recompense for the many camping and fishing expeditions we had to forego.

CONTENTS

iv

TABLES

FIGURES

CHAPTER I

SCOPE AND IMPORTANCE OF THE PROBLEM

Introduction

The term long-range planning has appeared only recently in management literature; however, since 1950 this term has appeared with increasing frequency. Early mention of the term can be traced back to periods prior to 1929. The concept of long-range planning probably existed in business circles long before businessmen and scholars began writing about it; within the military establishments long-range planning, as a concept and as a process of preparing for war, can be traced back to antiquity. Recent literature, while reflecting some writings on the subject, has failed to produce any which takes an integrated approach to the description of a philosophy of long-range planning.

During the past few years many companies have established full-time positions with a function variously referred to as "top management planning" or "long-range planning." The continuing establishment of these positions, with titles such as "Director of Planning," or "Manager of Corporate Planning," seems to indicate that a new differentiated and organic function of management is evolving in many United States corporations. In addition, professional management groups and colleges have developed informal discussion groups, composed of businessmen and scholars, to ponder the somewhat nebulous subject of long-term planning.

Although executive personnel have always performed a type of planning, it is only recently that American business has given serious consideration to the establishment of an organizational entity to develop tech-

1

niques, processes, procedures, and working assumptions for the performance of long-range planning. For example, in the past, men with titles such as "Assistant to the President," or "Executive Vice-President, Administration" have been concerned, at least on a part-time basis, with the general co-ordination of long-range planning. Reasons for the strong and growing interest of top executives in long-range planning are legion; however, despite the recent furor over long-range planning it is not dramatically new and revolutionary; it is perhaps a formalized extension of the decision-making process that is effected in any well-run business. The basic difference is that formal long-range planning encompasses greater time dimensions, more functional areas of effort, comprehensive extra-organizational considerations, and is conceived and managed in the institutional mind of the corporation rather than in the mind of any single executive.[1]

Abundant literature exists with respect to short-range planning, i.e., planning that is less than one year in duration. Both theory and practice have gone far in this respect. There is a large body of case experience containing sound generalizations and excellent insights. But, American industry and business is becoming more and more concerned with long-range objectives; current attention to long-range comparative rates of national economic growth between the United States and Russia appears to indicate this. In industry, some evidence exists to support the idea that management is giving greater attention to time horizons well beyond

---

[1]The term "institutional mind" as conceived by H. S. Person in the article, "On the Technique of Planning," *Bulletin of the Taylor Society of Industrial Engineers* (November, 1934) is one which can contemplate and conceptualize an idea independently of individuals within the organization. See pages 86 and 87 for a full discussion of this concept.

those to which they were previously accustomed. In addition, long-range planning has grown into a more or less formalized process covering a wider range of corporate interests than occurred in the past. As a result, the developing concept of long-range planning raises many issues and dimensions which are not answerable in terms of existing empirical and theoretical bases. Consequently, the need exists for a penetrating study of long-range planning, particularly as a developing philosophy within the existing management literature.

Long-range planning is conceived by the author as a type of planning for periods in excess of one year, which encompasses all functional areas of the business, and is effected within the existing and long-term future framework of economic, social, and technological factors. It is much more than a time dimension; it is a continuous process of broad scope which reflects a new way of thinking about the future, a new pattern of business and industrial life. It is a force making for the coordination of all the people, functions, effects, and extra-organizational factors of the corporate entity. It is developed on a scientific and objective basis drawn from a philosophy of management and from high ethical and social standards. Long-range planning is much more than business forecasting which involves trends and projections; it goes further by helping management to determine how to take advantage of the trends, how to minimize the effects of unfavorable trends, and how to attain full realization of the organization's service objectives.

In tracing the development of any thought attention should be given to an early understanding of the term philosophy and how a philosophy is developed. The philosophy of any subject is articulated as soon as its framework of principles, ideas, and practices has been given an

identifiable separateness and unity of its own; i.e., some momentum of
self-realized existence. For example, this has occurred in the fields
of history, science, medicine, law, and education. In each of these
cases, the progressive and comparative formulations of those informed
minds who have a generalizing inclination have brought new dignity and
significance to the subject and have also supplied it with an approach
and outlook which clarified relationships with other kindred subjects
and fields. A philosophy is the rational effort to answer the questions
of the widest generality conceivable posed about it. As Dimock conceives these questions:

> Why does this subject exist as a kind of entity in its own right?
> What is its area of activity and concern? To what purposes or
> ends does it direct itself? What general ideas or principles are
> regarded as controlling in respect to practice, the creation of
> new techniques, and evaluation? What kinds of methods are en-
> tailed in its operation and in its analytical phases? What are
> the norms, criteria, standards, by which sound judgments about
> activity within the field are to be determined?[2]

A philosophy, then, is a body of belief and practice aimed at achieving
better performance and includes a statement of the objectives toward
which the thought should be directed. As conceived by Davis a philosophy

> . . . is a system of thought based on some logical relationships
> between concepts and principles that explains certain phenomena
> and supplies a basis for rational solutions of related problems.
> A business philosophy is a system of thought that explains basic
> business problems and supplies the basis for an intelligent ap-

---

[2]Marshall E. Dimock, A Philosophy of Administration Toward Creative Growth (New York: Harper & Brothers, Publishers, 1958), p. viii.

proach to their solution. The philosophy of management is obviously the philosophy of business. It follows that scientific management requires a philosophy of management on which it can rest.[3]

Long-range planning, as a philosophy, obviously developed from an existing philosophy of management. This study is concerned with just why and how a philosophy of long-range planning developed in American business. As might be expected however, information about this subject is hard to find. Businessmen are generally reluctant to talk or write of their firms' long-range plans, which are usually closely guarded secrets; furthermore, long-range planning was, until after World War II, a relative rarity in business.

As mentioned earlier, the literature is lacking in an integrated study of long-range planning. In the course of the research for this dissertation no evidence was found of any attempt to trace the evolving concepts of long-range planning as reflected in historical literature nor was any study found which satisfied the requirement for a contemporary philosophy of long-range planning. Accordingly, the author has directed his efforts in the direction of developing a contemporary philosophy of long-range planning and in so doing of reflecting therein the historical derivation of such a philosophy.

Statement of the Problem

The purpose of this study was to isolate and trace the origin and development of a philosophy of long-range planning in American business. More specifically, this study is directed to an identification

---

[3]Ralph Currier Davis, The Fundamentals of Top Management (New York: Harper & Brothers, Publishers, 1951), pp. 6-7.

of the factors, forces, and environmental conditions that influenced certain American businesses to develop an internal philosophy of corporate long-range planning. In tracing this development several factors must be identified at the outset and considered as having significance throughout the study. These factors influence both the methodology and results of the effort. First, the paper is directed to tracing "an origin and development of a philosophy." This framework presupposes that both historical and contemporary influences are considered in order to present a complete picture of the problem. It must be recognized that any concept, philosophy, or cause did not develop in an environment devoid of time but did, rather, slowly evolve over a period of years into its present posture. Thus, the paper will treat both historical as well as contemporary aspects of the problem. This time-oriented approach will provide for the derivation and development of a contemporary American business philosophy of long-range planning which will establish a general policy, procedural, and organizational framework for long-range planning activities in an American business.

The further delineation of the problem requires a consideration of the following factors and interrogations:

1. What forces activated the requirement for long-range planning and facilitated its subsequent development in American business?

2. What has been the general development of a philosophy of long-range planning in American business from the period 1885 to the present time?

3. What long-range planning techniques, processes, policies, procedures, and devices are used by selected companies in selected segments of American business? What has been the result of long-range planning in American business?

4. What was the historical derivation of a concept of long-range planning into a philosophy?

5. How are companies organized for long-range planning activities? What is the general policy and procedural framework for effecting long-range planning? What specific functional areas of corporate effort are considered in these deliberations? What is the depth of effort in these areas? How far ahead do these businesses plan in these functional areas of effort?

6. Is there an identifiable philosophy of long-range planning in American business? If so, what is the extent of its application? What influences has it had upon the management of the business enterprise?

7. What internal and external factors are given consideration in American business long-range planning activities? What is the degree of participation in long-range planning by selected American businesses? How far ahead and generally how do selected companies approach the somewhat differentiated functional area of corporate long-range planning?

8. How are corporate long-range objectives established? How are long-range planning activities planned, organized, and controlled?

9. What type of forecasting is done to facilitate corporate long-range planning?

10. What corporate extra-organizational considerations are evaluated in this differentiated functional area of effort? How are data obtained for corporate long-range planning?

The foregoing framework constitutes a general perspective of the problem considered. The answers to these questions will perhaps, in turn, provide a general blueprint for use by a business in establishing a long-range planning effort within its organization. Secondly, this solution may provide for the identification of basic policies, factors, forces, and procedures to use in further sophisticating the existing long-range planning techniques of companies that have already developed some capability in this respect.

Importance of the Problem

An English economist, Alfred Marshall, begins Book V of his Principles of Economics as follows:

> A business firm grows and attains great strength, and afterwards perhaps stagnates and decays; and at the turning-point there is a balance or equilibrium, of the forces of life and decay.[4]

How to perpetuate the growth of a business enterprise and at the same time continue to provide a service to its customers is probably one of the chief objectives of scientific management. The life and health of a business enterprise is a function of many variables, some controllable. It is difficult to generalize about these many factors; it is, however, considered timely and provident to isolate the controllable factors, study them, and place such factors under as much corporate jurisdiction as possible. The recent attention given the subject of long-range planning is believed to be a factor which can be controlled, to some degree, by an enlightened corporate management.

H. L. Gantt, writing in 1919, said:

> It is thus clearly seen that the maintenance of our modern civilization is dependent absolutely upon the service it gets from the industrial and business system.[5]

---

[4]Alfred Marshall, Principles of Economics (8th edition; Macmillan & Co., Ltd.), p. 323.

[5]H. L. Gantt, Organizing For Work (New York: Harcourt, Brace & Howe and Co., Inc., 1919), p. 5.

The question arises, naturally, whether a business can give greater service if it is operated under a philosophy of management which contemplates a long-range planning function within its corporate activities. Recognition of the value of long-range planning and the subsequent employment of such techniques in the corporation can better prepare the enterprise for subsequent developments in its environment. This does not mean that the organization must tacitly accept its fate in the ensuing environment; it can, perhaps, favorably influence its future. In this respect Dr. Fred Polak develops a theory that the future of a civilization, a country, or a people is determined in large measure by its "images of the future."[6] He contends that it is possible to measure these "images of the future" and that it may be possible to alter or adjust them, thus to guide a nation's or people's future. According to Polak, if a society has optimistic ideas, dynamic aspirations, and cohesive ambitions, the civilization will grow and prosper. If it exhibits negative trends, uncertain ideals, and hesitant faith, then the society is in danger of disintegrating. The idea again is that by thinking about the future, man creates that same future according to his image. Does this thinking in the futurity have a place in business? Polak thinks the answer is yes. All of our great industrial enterprises grow on the strength of a leading image of the future whether these images be conscious or unconscious.

---

[6]Weldon B. Gibson, as cited in "Guideposts for Forward Planning," Long-Range Planning For Management, edited by David W. Ewing (New York: Harper & Brothers, 1958), pp. 488-489.

There has been increasing attention since World War II to the subject of long-range planning. An appreciable amount of periodical literature treating with specific aspects of the subject has appeared. These articles, for the most part, have been either philosophical in nature or have treated with the long-range planning activities of a specific company. A few books and ad hoc studies have appeared which represent a conglomeration of individual articles on the subject. Generally, information which attempts to integrate the myriad influences of long-range planning into a comprehensive document is practically non-existent. Since long-range planning is a relatively new concept, it is not surprising that as yet there has been no "classic" treatment of it in the literature. Furthermore, there apparently has been no attempt to pick up the historical evolving threads of thought on the subject and weave such into a contemporary philosophy.

The problem then becomes important, first, because of the growing prominence of the subject in American business, and secondly, because of the dearth of comprehensive and integrating information on the subject. It provides ample opportunity for primary research; furthermore, the author's position within the Air Force requires that he gain an appreciation of corporate long-range planning procedures and techniques in order that he might assist in refining and improving the performance of an important Air Force function, viz., advance weapons systems study and planning. Such learning as is assimilated in this study will be transferred to the Air Force for use by that organization in some of its activities. Thus the pursuit of the study has a purpose beyond satisfaction of degree requirements.

The subject of corporate long-range planning gains additional nota-
bility in light of the growing complexity of businesses, increasing domestic and foreign competition, and the acceleration of product obsolescence. The dynamics of the political, economic, and social surroundings
dictate that corporate management give attention to where the company is
headed. The growing influence of unions, society's desire for security
of employment, retirement, and for an increasing standard of living,
coupled with more and more government controls, precludes the business
enterprise from depending upon the "opportunity of chance" to provide for
a demand for its services. A recognition by business of the increasing
risk in business ventures and of the necessity of assuming even greater
risks has forced many businesses to undertake some semblance of long-range
planning in order to prepare better for the future. According to Drucker,

> The main goal of a management science must be to enable business
> to take the right risk. Indeed, it must be to enable business to
> take greater risks -- by providing knowledge and understanding of
> alternative risks and alternative expectations; by identifying
> the resources and efforts needed for desired results and by mobi-
> lizing energies for the greatest contribution; and by measuring
> results against expectations, thereby providing means for early
> correction of wrong or inadequate decisions.[7]

The early significance of corporate long-range planning is recognized by Henri Fayol in his writings. While he does not call this functional area of effort long-range planning per se, the long-term implication is very clearly recognized. He considers thinking out a plan and
insuring its success as one of the keenest satisfactions for an intelli-

---

[7]P. F. Drucker, "Thinking Ahead," Harvard Business Review (January, 1959), vol. 37, p. 146.

gent man to experience.[8] Fayol also recognizes the necessity of planning in his comment on the dangers threatening the business without a
plan, viz.,

> Lack of sequence in activity and unwarranted changes of course
> are dangers constantly threatening businesses without a plan.
> The slightest contrary wind can turn from its course a boat
> which is unfitted to resist. When serious happenings occur,
> regrettable changes of course may be decided upon under the in-
> fluence of profound but transitory disturbance. Only a programme
> carefully pondered at an undisturbed time permits of maintain-
> ing a clear view of the future and of concentrating maximum pos-
> sible intellectual ability and material resources upon the dan-
> ger.[9]

Another very significant factor points out the import of the problem, viz., the international situation where two fundamentally different
ideologies are in conflict. The need for further stabilization of the
American economy through individual corporate long-range planning may be
a favorable alternative over some type of future state planning which
would in all probability infringe on the prerogatives of private property
as it is presently envisioned in our contemporary society. Then too,
the very adverse result of another severe depression, such as this country experienced in the turbulent 30's, could be a fundamental change in
our form of government, and even in our way of life. Such an alternative would not be acceptable to American businessmen. It may very well
be that an acceptance by American business of a philosophy of long-range
planning will play an important role in moderating business fluctuations
directed towards aggregate economic stabilization and enhance the country's competitive position in the domestic and international markets.

---

[8]Henri Fayol, General and Industrial Management (London: Pitman,
1949), p. 39.

[9]Ibid., p. 49.

and techniques. The authors, in their conclusions, noted the significance of a company's future by stating:

> There is nothing about an organization more important than its future. Owners, management, employees, and society in general are, or should be, more concerned about where a company is going than where it has been. In any institution, the responsibility for visualizing, initiating, and achieving future objectives rests with its top management. The more specifically the future course of a company is conceived and defined, the more likely is its realization. One of the greatest needs observed during the course of this study is for more adequate planning and clarification of future objectives, both near-term and long-range.[12]

Henri Fayol's writings should be mentioned in any review of studies in long-range planning. While he apparently did not conduct a formal study per se, he did in his writings recognize the need for "prevoyance" in his recommendations for drawing up a plan of action in a large mining and metallurgical firm.

Business Week magazine in September, 1952, reported a survey whereby several large companies were briefly studied as to their long-range planning techniques. This study, conducted by the Business Week staff, reported the practices of seven corporations and concisely described the policy and procedural framework established for long-range planning. The general conclusions reached in this article were these:

1. More emphasis is being placed on systematic long-range planning by business.

2. Long-range planning is becoming a separate, specialized function of top management.

---

[12]Paul E. Holden, Launsbury S. Fish, and Hubert L. Smith. Top Management Organization and Control (Stanford University, California: Stanford University Press, 1941), p. 4.

3. Many variations exist as to the time period involved, with five years ahead as the usual range.[13]

Another study, similar to the above in its approach, was done by the National Industrial Conference Board in August of 1952. In this examination of the long-range planning activities of industrial companies some 151 corporations participated and provided answers to a questionnaire on long-range planning techniques. The study concluded that few standards existed regarding the activities to plan and the length of time for which plans should be devised. It was pointed out that the function of long-range planning was conducted somewhat formally; on the other hand some companies conducted it in a "somewhat haphazard manner."[14]

Many articles on long-range planning have appeared in periodical literature since the end of World War II. Before that period little attention was paid to the subject; the specific articles and their influence on the development of a philosophy of long-range planning are contained elsewhere in this dissertation. They do not fall into the category of ". . . previous studies," hence will not be reflected in this portion of the paper but will be integrated elsewhere. However, several significant articles have appeared recently which bear mention here. These articles are considered noteworthy particularly because they are more comprehensive and appeared in periodicals noted for their prestige in business

---

[13]"Business Probes Its Own Structure; Review of Planning and Developing the Company Organization Structure," Business Week (September 20, 1952), pp. 84-91.

[14]"Industry Plans For The Future," Conference Board Business Record, vol. 9 (August, 1952), pp. 324-328.

management literature. These articles are cited below along with a brief description of their contribution to the subject of long-range planning:

1. Ewing reviews the subject of long-range planning from an overall viewpoint, cites the experience of some companies in this area of effort, and discusses the theoretical aspects of the employment of the line and staff in long-range planning. Significantly the author recognizes that the existing literature of long-range planning is only a start as to what is needed in terms of authoritative books.[15]

2. The Stanford Research Institute, after a two-year initial study based on a review of the fortunes of about 400 companies from 1939 to 1957, concluded that successful growth companies have certain elements absent in less successful companies. These elements are --

   a. Forward-looking programs to promote the company's future in such areas as product development, company acquisitions, organization or management development, and operations research.

   b. Organized programs to seek and promote new business opportunities.

   c. An awareness on the part of the entire corporation of the significance of the planning function and broad participation in the business of planning even when the actual planning is done by economic staff groups.

Good management and especially sound planning methods are thought of as a means of improving a company's odds for success. A successful company is identified as one which has a forward looking program to promote its future.[16]

_____

[15]David W. Ewing, "Looking Around: Long-Range Business Planning," Harvard Business Review (July-August, 1956), pp. 135-146.

[16]"Why Companies Grow," Nation's Business (November, 1957), p. 2.

3. Bruce Payne reviews the steps involved in long-range planning, discusses the decision-making processes involved, and the procedures for developing long-range planning models.[17] Recognition is given to the need for a team approach in developing the plan. In his conclusions Payne establishes six basic questions to be answered in the development of a good plan.

a. Has the planning team determined the key influences in the growth of the industry and evaluated the influence of each?

b. Have the strengths and weaknesses of the company been accurately evaluated?

c. Have the capacities of different company functions to support the plan been projected far enough ahead?

d. Is there a practical timetable?

e. Have alternatives been considered?

f. What provisions have been made for future reverses?

4. H. Edward Wrapp reviews different modes of organization for long-range planning. Some suggestions, warnings, and lessons learned from company experience are reviewed and analyzed. The value of this study lies in the general model that can be deduced by a company that is approaching the task of setting up a long-range activity. He visualizes the type of management organization, the diversity of products, and the extent of previous budget research activity as probably the most important factors in deciding how to select a starting point for

---

[17]Payne, op. cit., pp. 95-106.

the planners. Top management support to the planning activity is recognized as a must; the development of a master plan for growth is viewed as a primary objective of the planning group.[18]

5. Platt and Maines discuss several alternative approaches that a company can use in developing experimental means by which to make its planning mistakes inexpensively. Several models and decision-making tools are briefly reviewed, such as operational models, business games, and ecological models. This study is unique inasmuch as it was the only such writing found which was devoted to the theme of testing long-range planning policies, procedures, and results. While they recognize that there may never be any all-embracing models in operations research that can be relied on to evaluate overall long-range company planning, the use of existing computer experimentation, business games, and ecological models can yield valuable test reports that can direct management toward better long-range plans.[19]

6. Quinn based his article on the results of a two-year study which included interviews with over 120 top-research, operating, and planning executives. The study, made under a grant from the Alfred P. Sloan Foundation, Inc., analyzes top-management questions and presents techniques that successful firms have used in planning their research programs. The article is aimed at placing technological planning in its

---

[18]H. Edward Wrapp, "Organization For Long-Range Planning," Harvard Business Review (January-February, 1957), pp. 37-47.

[19]William J. Platt and N. Robert Maines, "Pretest Your Long-Range Plans," Harvard Business Review (January-February, 1959), pp. 119-127.

proper perspective as part of top management's total planning activities.
In the article Quinn develops the key questions that a company must ask
itself when it is setting its long-range goals, viz.,

a. What business does the company want to be in? To stimulate
research top managers should look at the functions their products
perform, rather than the particular technique by which a product
achieves its purpose. Encourage non-traditional approaches to
problems.

b. What rate of growth is desirable? Company's financial capacities, management skills, market rigidities, etc. generally limit
the rate at which the company can realistically grow.

c. What overall direction does the intended growth take, e.g.,
vertically, horizontally, new fields or further penetration of
traditional markets, cyclical investments hedged by the company
entering countercyclical fields?

d. What method of growth is intended: acquisition, internal development, a combination of these approaches?

e. What is the company's desired image?

f. What other objectives should be considered? Percentage of
market to be held, degree of market flexibility, price-volume and
profit-volume markets the company wants to compete in, geographical
markets to be exploited, degree of decentralization, desired rate
of return on capital?[20]

---

[20]James Brian Quinn, "Long-Range Planning of Industrial Research,"
Harvard Business Review (July-August, 1961), pp. 88-102.

Books devoted wholly to long-range planning are even more difficult
to find than comprehensive periodical literature on the subject. Needless
to say, most of the contemporary books on management contain considerable
material on planning as an organic function of management. The minority
of the books reflect some discussion of long-range planning; none, to the
author's knowledge, recognize the existence of a philosophy of long-range
planning. Some individual books have appeared, however, which are edited
volumes of similar subject matter, viz.,

Bursk and Fenn edited a collection of papers from the proceedings
of the Twenty-Fifth National Business Conference sponsored by the Harvard
Business School Association. The articles, while not solely devoted to
strategic business planning, did emphasize long-range planning and its
place in the coming business world. The theme was covered in light of
particular company practices and experiences.[21]

In 1958 an anthology was published under the editorship of David
Ewing. A somewhat penetrating study of long-range planning, it discussed
organizing for planning and steps in making plans, forecasting, structur-
al change, operations research, computer applications, and manpower planning. Some problems were presented along with a suggestion of the limitations of long-range planning and the shortcomings of strategy formulation. Although it analyzed several of the more pertinent aspects of long-
range planning, the Ewing compendium did not formulate the long-range
planning problem in general. By its nature as a collection of individual
articles, the book lacked an integrated approach to the subject, and did
not analyze the requirements for an overall corporate approach to the so-

---

[21]Edward C. Bursk and Dan H. Fenn, Jr., (eds.), Planning The Future Strategy of Your Business (New York: McGraw-Hill Book Co., Inc.),
1956.

lution of long-term considerations. Another shortcoming of this book was
the fact that most of it was based on experience of businessmen; some
loss of depth resulted because of the failure of the editor to integrate
the theoretical aspects of long-range planning.[22]

Limitations of the Problem

The breadth of the subject of long-range planning requires as much
limitation as possible. Consequently, this paper is not concerned with
the detailed short-range planning activities of less than one year. This
rather arbitrary cut-off point is selected inasmuch as it appears that
most companies confine their short-range or operational planning to periods of less than one year. Some facets of a business organization are
concerned with routine day-to-day planning; the present study is concerned
with the element of futurity as a fundamental, far-reaching, and basic
corporate consideration evaluated at the top level of the organization.
The logic for excluding short-range planning from the study is that such
planning is, to a large degree, done at some organizational echelon below the top management level. In this respect Davis has said:

> As we go down the various organizational levels, approaching the
> point of primary operative performance, the required degree of
> futurity in planning decreases. Planning at the point of primary
> operative performance tends to be minor and involves practically
> no futurity.[23]

The study is restricted to a selected group of large corporations
representing an industry cross section of industrials. In addition,
large corporations from the life insurance, commercial banks, merchandis-

---

[22]David W. Ewing (ed.), Long-Range Planning For Management (New
York: Harper & Brothers, Publishers, 1958.

[23]Davis, op. cit., pp. 45-46.

ing, transportation, and public utilities fields of business effort are
examined. Only large corporations were contacted for questionnaire completion and/or study.

No attempt was made to evaluate the long-range planning techniques
of companies outside of the universe established above inasmuch as it is
assumed that only large corporations are likely to have a long-range planning effort, and, secondly, the sheer task of contacting more companies
than enumerated herein is beyond the scope of this study.

Specific computer, linear programming, mathematical, statistical,
and econometric techniques and processes as such were not investigated.
However, this is not meant to preclude the identification and general use
of such techniques as related to long-range planning activities in developing and solving the problem. The full development of these techniques
is not broached.

Periods prior to 1885 were not studied insofar as American business
long-range planning is concerned; however, military long-range planning
for periods prior to 1885 was briefly investigated in order to trace the
developing web of thought on long-range planning.

The study is concerned with long-range planning in business as opposed to any major considerations to other segments of the American society, such as social, military, economic, and government planning. The
general influences of these areas were investigated insofar as related
to long-range planning.

Although the functional areas of long-range planning were examined
briefly, no full development of the theoretical effort required in these
areas is attempted. Rather, the study is concerned with the functional
area as a part of a larger whole, not as an entity in long-range planning

itself. Furthermore, the types and extent of forecasts germane to the issue are scrutinized; no attempt is made to develop forecasting techniques in the finite sense because the development of forecasting activities becomes a function of the type of business, customer type, and other factors, and has no place in a paper such as this.

Definitions

Several important terms that are employed in this study require a specific definition in order to seperate them from the usual meaning of the term. In some instances even in management parlance the term may have several meanings; hence, precise selection of a pertinent connotation is believed appropriate. In a few cases Webster's definitions are given to insure the correct general usage of the term, both in the study and in the reader's frame of reference.

1. Philosophy: "A system of thought based on some logical relationships between concepts and principles that explains certain phenomena and supplies a basis for rational solutions of related problems. A business philosophy is a system of thought that explains basic business problems and supplies the basis for an intelligent approach to their solution."[24]

2. Long-range planning: "Planning based on a systematic effort to collect and analyze the significant economic, technological, political, social and market data needed as a basis for forecasting events and conditions one or more years in the future and then long-range planning out-

---

[24]Davis, op. cit., p. 6.

lines how the company will acquire and use economic resources to achieve its business goals and objectives in the forecast period."[25]

3. <u>Short-range planning</u>: "Planning based solely on routine reports and information flow or for a period of less than one year."[26]

4. <u>Concept</u>: "A thought, an opinion; an idea, as distinguished from a percept; especially as originated, an idea representing the meaning of a universal term and comprehending the essential attributes of a class or logical species; an idea that includes all that is characteristically associated with, or suggested by, a term; also, a mental image of an action or thing."[27]

5. <u>Origin</u>: "The fact or process of coming into being from a source; derivation; beginning regarded in connection with its cause; parentage, ancestry, that from which anything primarily proceeds; source, fountain; spring; cause."[28]

6. <u>Plan</u>: "A specification of the factors, forces, effects, and relationships that enter into and are required for the solution of a business problem."[29]

---

[25] E. Miller, "Long-Range Planning: Overview," <u>Advanced Management</u> (November, 1960), p. 8-11.

[26] Ibid., p. 11.

[27] William Allan Neilson (ed.), <u>Webster's New International Dictionary of The English Language</u> (second edition, unabridged; Springfield, Mass.: G. & C. Merriam Company, Publishers, 1960), p. 552.

[28] Ibid., p. 1720.

[29] Davis, <u>op. cit.</u>, p. 43.

7. <u>Master Plan</u>: A specification of the total corporate and extra-organizational factors, forces, effects, and relationships to be consider-ed in developing a future posture for the business organization.

Methodology Used in Developing the Study

The first major step in the study was to conduct a comprehensive review of existing literature on the subject of long-range planning. A prime purpose of this review was to become knowledgeable in the area, to provide input into the author's frame of reference for the development of the questionnaire, and to begin the rudimentary concepts and philoso-phy under which the study was to be pursued. Another important aspect of the literature review was to identify the primordial aspects of long-range planning thought and to trace these thoughts into the evolving philosophy that was expected to develop as the literature approached contemporary times. General understanding of the subject was gained also through this review; it also provided an indication of the originality of the subject and the approach.

The largest amount of information came from periodicals; books on the subject, as heretofore mentioned, were limited to a few edited col-lections of writings. The periodical literature reviewed was taken from the indexes as follows:

1. Industrial Arts Index -- 1913 to present

2. Air University Index -- 1945 to present

3. Reader's Guide to Periodical Literature -- 1900-1914

4. 19th Century Reader's Guide to Periodical Literature -- 1890-1899

5. Poole's Index to Periodical Literature -- 1887-1892

6. Wall Street Journal Index -- all Indexes

In addition to the foregoing, general management textbooks were reviewed. While these books did provide abundant writing on planning, in general, little information suitable for use in this study was found. However, the military history books did provide some input into the military aspects of long-range planning. An analysis of the availability of both periodical and book literature on the subject is reflected in a previous section.

The recency of development of long-range planning activities in American business is reflected in the dearth of integrating information on the subject. Hence, primary research became the main method of data collection for the study. In terms of primary data collection several methods were concurrently utilized:

1. Preparation and distribution of a comprehensive questionnaire. The specific details of the preparation, validation, and distribution of this document will be discussed in a subsequent portion of the present section.

2. In addition to the foregoing the author personally conducted intensive interviews and study with two corporations located in and in close proximity to Dayton, Ohio. Also, one other company in an area remote to Dayton, Ohio, was studied. This remote study was conducted on an "opportunity" basis compatible with the author's travels as a production and procurement staff officer in the Air Force. The author's position responsibilities within the Air Force precluded any extensive absence from military duties, hence key reliance was placed on the questionnaire as a source of primary research data.

Considerable time and effort were devoted to the development of a suitable questionnaire. In the initial stages, extensive notes were taken during the literature review. These notes were condensed and structured into suitable questions concerning long-range planning for incorporation into the first draft. This initial draft was discussed in detail with the adviser, fellow students, and with professional associates. After several revisions, the questionnaire began to develop into a form suitable for field testing. The field test indicated that some revisions were required, consequently the questionnaire was restructured, shortened, and developed into a logical sequence of relationships into what appeared to the author to be the entire spectrum of corporate long-range planning activities:

1. Long-Range Planning Policy

2. Derivation of Long-Range Planning Need

3. Planning Period Determinants

4. Organization for Long-Range Planning

5. Functional Areas of Long-Range Planning

6. Extra-organizational Considerations in Long-Range Planning

7. Long-Range Planning Procedures and Techniques

8. Long-Range Planning Processes

9. Long-Range Planning Results

Final validation of the questionnaire into its present form was accomplished by working closely with personnel in the market research and long-range planning office of two large, integrated companies located in Dayton, Ohio. The counsel and assistance rendered by these agencies assisted materially in the development of both the questionnaire and the sampling techniques.

After the questionnaire evolved into a "near final form," it was again dispatched on another field test. Of ten copies forwarded three were returned with answers that could be used satisfactorily in the study. The number of favorable responses was considered high enough to justify releasing the main body of questionnaires. The final form taken by the questionnaire is reflected in the Appendix.[30] Questionnaires were then dispatched to 225 large American corporations as follows:[31]

Industrials	150
Commercial Banks	15
Life Insurance Companies	15
Merchandising Firms	15
Transportation Companies	15
Utilities	15
Total	225

The industrials were selected, insofar as possible, from industry grouping classifications established by the Bureau of the Budget, viz.,

Food and Beverage
Autos, Aircraft, Shipbuilding
Appliances, Electronics
Rubber
Polishing and Printing
Lumber and Wood Products
Metal Products
Textiles
Machinery
Chemicals
Tobacco
Paper and Allied Products
Metal Manufacturing
Glass, Cement, Gypsum, Concrete
Petroleum Refining

---

[30]See Appendix B.

[31]For the purpose of this study, a large American business is defined as one having the following attributes:
    Industrials: Annual sales above $70,000,000.
    Commercial Banks: Assets above $585,000,000.
    Life Insurance Co's.: Assets above $228,211,000.
    Merchandising Firms: Annual sales above $190,000,000.
    Transportation Co's.: Operating revenues above $68,180,000.
    Utilities: Assets above $380,000,000.

All businesses solicited were selected from the "500 Largest Industrials" and the "50 Largest Commercial Banks, Life Insurance Companies, Merchandising Firms, Transportation Companies and Utilities" reflected in Fortune magazine (July-August, 1961).[32] The corporations were selected from a grouping categorized on the basis of Total Sales (Industrials, Merchandising Firms), by Assets (Commercial Banks, Life Insurance Companies and Utilities), and by Operating Revenues (Transportation Companies). Finite categorization and information gathering techniques are explained in the Appendix.[33]

The questionnaire was sent personal to the president or appropriate vice-president based on names selected from Poor's Register of Executives.[34] It is believed that this technique elicited a more favorable response than would have resulted in simply sending the questionnaire to the company without specific direction to any one corporate official.

It was assumed at the time of distribution of the questionnaire that at least forty per cent of the businesses solicited would respond favorably and provide information suitable for use in the dissertation. Based on this assumption 225 businesses polled would have resulted in usable information from ninety companies which would represent a cross section of large American businesses. Chapter IV explains the response that was actually received from the questionnaire distribution.

Without question, the establishment of the criteria for the corporations to be interviewed and sent questionnaires was somewhat arbitrary.

---

[32] "The Fortune Directory," Fortune (July, 1961), pp. 167-186; "The Fortune Directory," Fortune (Part II, August, 1961, pp. 129-138.

[33] See Appendix A.

[34] Poor's Register of Directors and Executives (New York: Standard and Poor's Corporation, 1961), selected pages.

However, insofar as possible this was done randomly within the framework
of sales and industry categorizations. Statistical exactness was not desired nor possible in this study because of the nebulous nature of long-
range planning, the myriad alternatives possible of selection in the
study, and the spatial and time limits imposed. Rather, it was intended
to gather information from an adequate number of large American businesses
to determine whether a philosophy of long-range planning did exist in the
contemporary business world. No attempt was made to develop sampling
formulas to use in gathering the information. The study was not predicated upon a statistical basis; rather the information was gathered in
as scientific a manner as possible but yet at the same time avoiding
purely statistical methodology.

CHAPTER II

MILITARY EVOLUTION AND CONCEPT OF LONG-RANGE PLANNING

Influence of the Military Staff

Military leaders began writing about line and staff concepts long before such ideas were accepted by the business world; military staffs were conceived and employed in antiquity. As is its civilian counterpart, the staff agency in the military establishment is set up for the purpose of providing the commander, and the heads of the other staff departments, with certain specialized assistance. A staff officer, whether in the military establishment or in business, is an adviser; an extension of the personality and authority of the line official whom he serves. The duty of the staff individual is to assist the executive, by giving recommendations which will facilitate and coordinate the activities of all the subfunctions. One authority has conceived of the staff function of consisting of two principal types and groups, i.e., technical staff and coordinative staff. The first provides assistance in creative planning or supplies some technical staff service or facilitation. The coordinative staff agencies assist in controlling operations and the coordination of action.[1] The general staff, as a concept of military organization, is concerned with the long-range creative planning that is required to develop plans for the employment of the national military forces.

---

[1] R. C. Davis, "What The Staff Function Actually Is," *Advanced Management* (May, 1954), p. 16.

The staff function in the military organization began with individual staff services and eventually evolved into a departmentalized and
coordinative staff service. The influence of the military staff has been
significant in the business world. In this respect Alvin Brown remarks:
"Indeed the idea of staff is so closely identified with military organization that the latter may be considered possessor of the copyright."[2]
While the modern concept of the army general staff is usually traced to
the seventeenth century, when emphasis was placed upon a top staff of
experts by Gustavus Adolphus of Sweden, such a function as the general
staff performed apparently was not recognized and practiced by business
organizations until a much later period. As industry began to develop
its own concept of a general staff type of organization, most of the
planning work given to such an entity was short range in nature. It is
problematical whether business will ever develop an organization which
operates as completely under the general staff concept as does the military general staff. However, some evidence in business seems to indicate
that performance of a long-range planning function has been assigned to
organizational structures which have a philosophy of management, similar
to that employed by the military general staff. The question naturally
arises whether there has been any parallel development between the business form of a general staff type of organization, and the evolving philosophy of long-range planning. Later sections of this study will probe
this question to see if such a relationship does exist.

---

[2]Alvin Brown, Organization, A Formulation of Principle (New York:
Hibbert Printing Company, 1945), p. 277.

Contemporary Concept of the Military General Staff

The term general staff has had various uses and often designates the staff of a general commanding any major unit of division size or greater; it most commonly denotes the staff of the central headquarters directing the nation's entire military establishment. The general staff in peace time is concerned with the training and administrative control of existing forces and with the preparation of plans for any war in which the nation might become involved.

A general staff in the modern sense means a completely organized informative, advisory, and supervisory staff service, including every general function pertaining to such a service, all coordinated under one head, the chief of staff. A general staff function means a staff service so general and constant in its character that it constitutes a continuous necessity to the organization as a whole. The armies of the North and South, that fought the Civil War, had in their organizations no coordinated general staff in the present-day sense, but they had general staff services, meaning staff functions that were constant and necessary to the whole organization. Modern general staff organization coordinates all such services. The general staff is not an agency for operations; rather it is a staff planning and supervising agency. It acts as an overall agency, ensuring adequate coordination and effectiveness according to the plan.

It would be reasonable to say that through history, the principles of military organization and management have served as guideposts to many of the current problems of industrial organization and management. The industrial organization, by partitioning the phases of responsibility, particularly that of planning, also stemmed undoubtedly from Tayler's idea of functional foremanship with overtones of emulation of the military theory of staff.[3] The widespread use of staff agencies in American business developed only in the twentieth century, particularly after the great depression. An implicit relationship exists between the military general staff developed for long-term planning and the evolving philosophy of long-range planning in business. What this relationship is will be reflected in the present chapter; also, a study and discussion of how such a general staff developed in the military organization will be afforded.

Influence of the Military General Staff Concept

The origin and development of many organization practices and procedures used by business can be directly traced to the military establishment. It has been suggested that the military general staff, as a peacetime long-range planning center, was conceived in antiquity and reached its fullest development with the refinement given it by the German Army. The value of a study of evolution of the general staff has special import, inasmuch as such a staff agency developed and practiced the fundamentals of long-range planning long before any application of long-range planning was given to business. The success of the German General Staff, as a peace-time planning center, is manifest in the employment of the plans that such staff developed during the first and second World Wars. Within the military establishment, the general staff was created and refined in order to provide a peace-time planning center for the conduct of future operations. The creation of such an agency permitted the commanders to adjust their war plans according to the influences developed by the general staff.

---

[3]Ibid., p. 164.

The development of long-range planning concepts in the military organization closely parallels the evolving philosophy of the employment of a military staff agency. The staff, on the other hand, was created and employed because of the increasing complexity of preparing for and conducting war, first, on a national and international scale, and more recently on a global basis. Recent successful penetrations into outer space hints that future wars may very well encompass an entire universe, or at least be interplanetary in nature with a commensurate increase in pre-planning activities.

The growing complexity of war over the centuries is reflected in the increasing amount of pre-planning that was necessary in order to plan for, organize, and control the large employment of men, weapons, and materials necessary to conduct a successful campaign. When primitive men fought, few weapons were required, little pre-planning was necessary, and combat was probably spontaneous, dependent for its outbreak on the belligerent attitude of the participants. As long as warfare remained so simple little requirement existed for a staff to provide advice and counsel and to conduct what limited planning was necessary for primitive men to band together for self-protection and mutual assistance. Logistics, intelligence, and management of large forces were not a consideration; any basic plans that evolved probably were arrived at as an expedient of the moment and did not have any significant time dimensions.

In attempting an historical approach to any phase of military development, it is difficult to arrive at certain conclusions and relate these conclusions to certain periods; obviously some periods have been more fruitful than others. Some eras have witnessed great contributions

to military thought, while others have been barren. In this respect,
Colonel Hittle, writing on the development of the military staff, has
said:

> Generally, productive military thought in an era has evolved si-
> multaneously with cultural and scientific progress. It is para-
> doxical, but true, that the periods which have contributed most
> to the development of civilization have also contributed the
> means by which mankind could more efficiently engage in mass
> killing.[4]

Early evolution of the staff agency, as an instrument of military
planning, is difficult to isolate because its early development is obscured in unwritten history and the informalities of early warfare.
Many great victories attributed to a single military genius may have
been possible only because of meticulous thinking (or planning) on the
part of a competent staff. If major military forces were employed, no
single military genius had sufficient knowledge of the entire situation
to conduct the long-range planning necessary to the successful conduct
of the campaign. While doubtlessly the supreme commander did establish
basic and long-term plans for the operation, such was done only after
the advice and counsel of his staff had been taken into consideration.

The nature of primitive staff planning is veiled in obscurity;
however, it should be recognized that the absence or presence of legis-
tical support is the deciding factor in determining the organizational
advancement of a military force of any significant size. The existence
of a planning function for supply and quartering presupposes the actual
or contemplated existence of a force of sizeable proportions. The degree of planning, and whether it becomes projected far enough into the

[4]J. D. Hittle, The Military Staff, Its History and Development
(Harrisburg: The Military Service Publishing Co., 1949), p. 10.

future to be called long-range planning, becomes a function of the size
of the force, the geographical area of employment, and the time factor
involved. Thus, in the evolving philosophy of war, as it became more
national and international in scope, long-range planning, in the sense
envisioned in this paper, became a necessity. This can perhaps be better presented by reviewing some ancient military campaigns to see if logistics type long-range planning did in fact exist.

The Evolution of Military Planning Staffs

History tells of the campaigns of the Assyrians who conducted seige
operations which compared favorably with techniques employed as late as
the Middle Ages. The planning and executing of the engineering of seige
operations must have required some fairly advanced planning. Certainly
any army that conducted such far-flung conquests as did the Assyrians
must have had a highly sophisticated logistic planning function. Some
evidence exists that they utilized arsenals and storehouses for providing logistic support to the campaigning troops. Other single examples
of military history tend to lead one to the conclusion that a long-range
planning concept did evolve with military strategy; to cite a few:

1. The campaigns of Darius, extending from the Punjab to the
regions of the Don could only have been accomplished upon the basis of
careful preparation. Xenophon (Greek historian-soldier, 435-355 b.C.),
in writing of Darius, said campaigns near seacoasts were supplied by
ships, and that there were transports for men and horses. The coordination of land and sea operations certainly implies the existence of a
planning function extending appreciably into the future.

2. Phillip, father of Alexander the Great, created a staff system which was able to support the wide-spread campaigns of his son. Missile throwing weapons, seige operations, and fortifications were developed along with a commissary and transport organization. Alexander, after his father's death, commanded one of the greatest military machines in all history through thirteen years of continuous campaigns that extended all over the known world.

3. The conquests of the Roman Armies, and the wide areas of military occupation conducted by Caesar's legions, were dependent upon a highly efficient staff organization, particularly in the function of planning. Caesar had "quaestors" who functioned as supply officers. The quaestor appears to be the functional origin of the term "quartermaster," which in later military history, particularly in the German General Staff, becomes concerned with long-range operational planning.

After the fall of the Roman Empire military knowledge and its practice seemed to disappear, especially in the sense of the further refining of staff and planning procedures. Even the crusades, while extending over a period of some two centuries, and producing a number of "soldiers of fortune," did not add much to the strategy of arms employment. Certainly the claim should not be made that all long-range planning disappeared as a function of a staff agency; rather, it appears to have happened that a "rough and ready" staff system was employed. Hittle, writing on the history and development of the military staff, claims that modern military management and development began after the beginning of the fourteenth century.[5]

---

[5]Ibid., pp. 27-29.

Much of the credit for subsequent development of the staff, particularly
in logistic planning, is credited to Gustavus Adolphus, particularly
since he, probably more than any other individual, was responsible for
the development of organized supply systems within the army. This necessary planning for logistics disappeared entirely from military thinking after the disintegration of the Roman Armies and was not fully re-
established until Gustavus revitalized it.[6]

With the departure of Gustavus and his military genius from the
scene in Europe, contemporary armies began to modify the staff system
promulgated by the great Swede. It underwent modifications to suit the
particular country's need. The basic purpose of the staff remained,
however, viz., "thinking out" the detail and planning for ensuing campaigns. The first emergence of a long-range planning function in ancient
armies can be related to a function of an organized staff service and
performing an organic necessity common to all armies, large or small,
viz., castramentation, or the laying out of a military camp. The planning for such places, safe and suitable, whether the army is in the immediate presence of the enemy, is a scouting function, inherent in the
informative phase of staff service. It seems to be a legitimate inference that the duties of the quartermaster grew out of the scouting duties even as the duties of the chief of staff have evolved out of those
of the quartermaster. These duties, when performed during short campaigns required short-range planning, but as the breadth of the plan of
war increased, the planning became increasingly longer term, especially

---

[6]Ibid., pp. 34-36.

as economic and social considerations, a factor of war, began to gain in
import. During the late Seventeenth and Eighteenth centuries most of
the European armies expanded greatly and the duties of the quartermaster
were broadened until that officer took on many of the duties that today
fall under the purview of the general staff whose responsibilities, it
should be noted, include the coordination of both short and long-range
planning activities in the military establishment.

Development of the German General Staff

In 1801 one Gerhard Johann Scharnhorst applied to the King of
Prussia for employment in the Prussian Army. Scharnhorst became the
educator of a new generation of officers in the Prussian Army, and in
January and November, 1802, under his guidance, two important documents
were drawn up and issued by the Prussian staff. These memoranda pointed
out the necessity of a permanent general staff which was to function as
a peace-time planning center. The memorandums proposed that even in
time of peace operational plans for every conceivable military eventuality should be prepared. Thus two fundamental concepts seem to have
been born, first, the general staff idea, and second, the acceptance of
the need for a formal organizational entity devoted to developing long-
range plans for the employment of the national military establishment
in furtherance of political and ideological aims. It is considered significant to note that this organization, the embryonic general staff,
was primarily concerned with the planning function and was accordingly
organized along these lines. Later circumstances and philosophies
changed the organization from what was originally envisioned in the
early 1800 memorandums, but basically the concept of planning remained
and the planning activity continued to be the fulcrum from which future

military operations were investigated, evaluated, and tested.[7] Unquestionably this new organization was concerned with a myriad of details appropriate to the employment of an army and navy; such details being both short and long range in their implications for the development of "every conceivable military eventuality." Such responsibilities certainly must have contemplated the preparation of strategic plans extending well into the future and encompassed military, economic, and social considerations. The coordination and integrating function incidental to the development of these plans required a sizeable staff which deliberated in much abstract thought to develop alternative approaches and methods of troop employment. The peacetime function of the staff was thus fundamentally in the preparation for the next war and the drawing up of appropriate plans thereof. Such functions have become the practice of most general staff agencies in the military world.

Most scholars of military science considered the German General Staff as a model for subsequent staff development throughout the military world. An indication of the importance of the German General Staff as a peace-time long-range planning organization is hinted at during the negotiations for the Peace Treaty in Versailles. Here, the German peace delegates found that one of the Allied provisions in the Treaty was the reduction of the German Army to 100,000 men, universal military service was to be abolished, and the General Staff forbidden. The Treaty did not forbid the Truppengeneralstab (Operational General Staff). This agency's chief of operations, by name one Wetzel, instructed an assis-

---

[7]Walter Goerlitz, History of the German General Staff (New York: Praeger, Inc., 1953), pp. 3-14.

tant to ". . . at least save the kernel of the 'fine and nobly conceived institution of the Great General Staff' and transplant it in some form or other into the new army."[8] The spirit of the German General Staff was preserved, for in the reorganization following the Treaty of Versailles there was created the Truppenant or "Troop Officer," which carried on what had hitherto been the work of the general staff.[9] The manifold examples of German successes in the Second World War is testimony to the success that the general staff had in subsequent years. At the reopening of the Kriegsakademie in October 1935 the principles of the General Staff's work was formulated in a speech by Ludwig Beck, Chief of the General Staff, as "First, logical and systematic thought, careful working out of all situations . . . then after good planning, decisive action."[10]

In spite of the infamous reputation of the German General Staff there appears to be ample evidence that Hitler did not allow it to exercise its full theoretical position in the Third Reich. In fact, in the later years of World War II he relegated it to a position of simply providing technical assistance and did not use it as a planning agency, especially in terms of long-range planning. The accusation made against the General Staff before the International Court in Nuremberg that it was one of the organizations that had played a leading part in unleashing the Second World War was found impossible to sustain.[11] However, had the staff been permitted to play a full part in operational planning the outcome of the war and guilt for perpetrating the world conflict might have been different.

---

[8]Ibid., p. 212. [9]Ibid., p. 218. [10]Ibid., p. 295. [11]Ibid., p. 499.

The peculiarities of employing vast quantities of men and materials in conflict mothered the development of a specialized organizational element to perform a planning function and to coordinate a subsequent implementation of the plans. The many alternatives of selection in such situations breed the necessity for a staff planner. Clausewitz has said in speaking of a plan of war:

> . . . and now see on the other hand, the immense number of circumstances which present themselves for consideration to the investigating mind; the long, often indefinite distances into which the threads of the subject spin out and the number of combinations which lie before us.[12]

Clausewitz foresaw that the plan of war comprehends the whole military operation and that through development and employment of the plan the operation becomes a single act.

The General Staff in the United States

In the United States there was little evidence of a general staff to do long-range planning for the Civil War. Whatever may have been McClellan's short-comings as a field commander, there was one point in which he demonstrated a military wisdom that placed him far above his contemporaries. Upon finding that the traditional staff system was not suitable for such a large command as had been given him, he made some changes, which were a start in bringing the Northern staffs in line with the more advanced European doctrine of the times, viz., assumption of planning function and development of both short and long-range plans for the army of the Potomac.[13]

---

[12]Karl von Clausewitz, On War. Translated from the German by O. J. Matthijis Jolles (Washington, D.C.: Infantry Journal Press, 1943), p. 568.

[13]J. G. Harvar, "The American General Staff," The Saturday Evening Post (March 13, 1936), p. 51.

The long period of peace in the United States brought sleepy oblivion to the need for a military staff and for a strategic study of the long-range employment of the armed forces. The size of the Army and Navy was reduced and the War Department reorganized so that any attempt at co-ordinated and comprehensive development of war plans was an impossibility. The pursuit of the Spanish-American War pointed out forcibly the critical requirement for a peace-time planning agency in the War Department. Fortunately, the Spanish resistance crumbled so rapidly that the Army did not face any severe military test. However, the utter confusion that resulted in the mobilization and outfitting of the Army pointed up vividly the need for a reorganization of the military establishment along the lines of a general staff so that planning for future emergencies could be effected.[14] It is significant to note that it was to the German General Staff that the United States turned after 1898 when it was decided to modernize our military system.

Elihu Root, Secretary of War during the reorganization of the Army, conceived of the United States General Staff as a body which was to devote its energies to both planning and coordination. For instance, in his annual report of 1902, Secretary Root emphasized the planning of the General Staff by stating:

> It (the General Staff) is not an executive body; it is not an administrative body; it acts only through the authority of others. It makes intelligent command possible by procuring and arranging information and working out plans in detail, and it makes intelligent and effective execution of commands possible by keeping all the separate agents advised of the parts they are to play in the General Scheme.[15]

---

[14] Major General Otto L. Nelson, Jr., National Security and The General Staff (Washington: Infantry Journal, 1946), pp. 1-10.

[15] Ibid.

The military general staff agency had its inception in antiquity and has evolved slowly over the centuries into its present, highly refined structure capable of providing, among other things, the long-range planning necessary to the employment of a military global striking force. In its beginnings, obscured in the veil of time, it doubtlessly performed routine planning necessary to the immediate campaign ahead. As wars became more complex and extended over a greater time period, the staff engaged in planning which extended over a greater distance into the future. In modern times general staff planning is projected many years into the future and plans are formulated within an ideological and military framework which encompasses total commitment of a nation's resources. The military staff, it may reasonably be inferred, developed the first conceptual rudiments of long-range planning of any sort. The evolving concept of long-range planning in the military establishment seems to have developed somewhat concurrently with the creation of a separate staff agency to assist in the formulation of national military objectives. Evidence suggests that the military concept of the development of long-term objectives, and the establishment of plans to reach such objectives, was accepted and used widely by military groups long before such an image was recognized and developed in the business world. This has been particularly so in the United States where a strong popular feeling has existed that military people are necessarily rigid and incompetent. This feeling was transferred from Great Britain to the United States, and the War of Independence strengthened it. The drafters of the Constitution were especially careful to provide safeguards to preclude the possibility of the military establishment gaining too much authority in the national government.

Present day organization of the Defense Department of the Federal Government places civilian secretaries in authority over the military forces which seems to indicate that even present day legislators fear the development of too much power by military personnel. One only need review the Congressional hearings conducted during the 1898-1902 study of the General Staff concept for the United States to realize the strong public sentiment against a potent general staff.

This inherent fear of the military organization by civilian components in the United States may very well have stifled the acceptance by businessmen of the military philosophy of long-range planning and the transferring of such planning policies and procedures to the business world. Dale and Urwick hint that an influence making for distrust of military forms of organization among businessmen may have been the writings of Taylor. His development of "functional foremanship" is described as a replacement for the "military form of organization."[19] In describing as "military" the then existing system, in American machine shops by which the foreman was a jack-of-all-trades, Taylor was inaccurate. What he apparently had in mind was the authoritarian character of military discipline rather than a form of military organization. By using such a term as "military" Taylor reinforced the prejudice against military forms of organization in American business.[20]

Probably the resource requirements of waging total war on a global basis which occurred during World War II motivated a closer relationship

[19]Ernest Dale and Lyndall F. Urwick, Staff In Organization (New York: McGraw-Hill Book Company, Inc., 1960), p. 58.

[20]Ibid., p. 60.

of the military and civilian components in the government structure. The
unprecedented development of the productive capacities of the United
States industry to meet the demands of the war fostered mutual military-
civilian management effort in war industries; the inadequate plans of industry for increasing its productive powers was pointedly identified at
the start of hostilities. Any form of distrust of military organization
or methods was subordinated to the all demanding requirement for rapid
production of the materials of war. Military long-range plans were in
being but were delayed in becoming operational because of the lack of
the necessary logistical support. As will be developed later in the
paper this point may have been a decisive one, for industry fully realized, perhaps for the first time, the need for the acceptance of a philosophy of long-range planning. Events subsequent to World War II intensi-
fied this philosophy, particularly in view of the uneasy East-West stale-
mate and the Korean conflict. Post-Korea military leaders, faced with
the task of sustaining a large military force in being for an undetermin-
able period in the future, began effecting long-range planning on an unprecedented scale. Russian aims for world communism and the international
race for space exploitation and domination dictates commitment of America's
national resources on long-range plans some of which may be irrevocable.
General Schreiver, Commander, Air Force Systems Command, United States Air
Force, best described the long-range planning problem of the military
forces by stating:

. . . Moreover, the advent of the Space Age is extending the area and scope of operations that can be used by a potential enemy. All of these factors demand that we gear our management to the long-range task of providing the systems we need for defense.[21]

Credit for the initial recognition and acceptance of a long-range planning philosophy must be given to the military establishment. This comes about, in all probability, because of the maturation of the military general Staff, a unique organization created to perform a specific function for military and political leaders, viz., planning the strategy of war. Whatever caused businessmen to neglect accepting this military innovation is debatable; however, the concept of long-range planning is a birth-right of the military, both in inception and in employment.

---

[21]Speech given by General Schriever, Bernard A., Commander, Air Force Systems Command, as reported in Armed Forces Management (February, 1962), p. 40. Title of article, "The Real Challenge To Military Management."

CHAPTER III

EARLY DEVELOPMENT OF A PHILOSOPHY OF LONG-RANGE PLANNING
IN AMERICAN BUSINESS

Introduction

In tracing the early development of a philosophy of long-range
planning in American business several preliminary concepts and factors
must be briefly investigated in order to lay a proper framework for the
ensuing evolution of thought. Planning, as a word in the English language, had a specific meaning and it was modified to suit the changing
environment in which it was used. The forces which influenced changes
in the word "plan" were an outgrowth of the planning process as viewed
by scholars and practitioners during the development of the word into
its present connotation. A brief review of this process, as well as the
concept of social, economic, military, and industrial planning will be
given in this chapter.

Developing a framework of thought which reflects the evolving
philosophy of long-range planning has been accomplished in this chapter,
using the following organization:

Early Long-Range Planning Rudiments (1880-1900)

Evolution of Long-Range Planning Images (1900-1930)

Recognition of the Need for Long-Range Planning in American
Business (1930-1940)

The Expansion of Long-Range Planning Concepts (1940-1950)

The following chapters will discuss the contemporary philosophy of long-
range planning in American business and will encompass events, factors,

50

forces, and effects of the time period 1950-1961. The final chapter will
be devoted to a summary and conclusion of the study effort.

The foregoing organization has been given to reflect the evolving
philosophy of long-range planning. The evolving thought on the subject
has been a recent phenomenon; consequently some of the early periods do
not reflect a great amount of thinking on the subject.

Derivation of a Planning Concept

When the word "plan" entered the English language, it had a highly
refined meaning. It was derived from the Latin _planus_, connoting "flat"
and is etymologically the same word as "plane." The _Oxford_ _English_ _Dic-_
tionary attempts to present the words that have formed the English vocabu-
lary from the time of the earliest records down to the present day with
all the relevant facts concerning their form, sense-history, pronuncia-
tion, and etymology. The derivation of a word refers to the formation or
development of a term from its original elements and refers also to the
tracing of this process. This type of examination not only gives an idea
of how the word developed but also gives a good indication of the development of the concept which the word connotes. In this respect the word
plan is defined and dated as to usage thusly:

> To devise, contrive, design (something to be done, or some action
> or proceeding to be carried out); to scheme, project, arrange be-
> forehand. . . . 1737 Pope Hor. Epist. II. e. 374. We needs will
> write Epistles to the king; . . . Be called to Court to plan some
> work divine. 1782 Miss Curney Celcilia V. XI., Cecelia the whole
> time was planning how to take her leave. . . . 1868 Freeman, Nor-
> man Conquest. II. X. 470. Never was a campaign more ably planned.[1]

---

[1] The Oxford English Dictionary, Volume VII, N-Poy (Oxford: The
Clarendon Press, 1933), pp. 941-942.

Earlier use of the word in English (1678) describes a drawing or sketch made by projecting an object on a plane surface; apparently it was something similar to a "blueprint." Contemporary meanings of the word "plan" and its gerund have evolved into a broader meaning in business and industry from its early narrow connotation. Nevertheless the planning in business and government still retains much of its Seventeenth century meaning of a drawing or sketch. A fundamental difference is that the early usages of the word and its derivatives treated with things and people; current connotations of the word contemplate people, things, ideas, concepts, abstractions, ideologies, and philosophies. Whereas early usage of the term apparently did not reflect time dimensions, present employment of the word, especially in business and industry, considers definite time concepts as revealed in the use of the terms long range and short range.

Planning today in American business is recognized by most authorities in the field of management as an organic function which precedes the collateral organic functions of organizing and controlling. Some writers have gone further and broken down controlling into derivative organic functions, viz., coordinating and directing. There is, however, little disagreement among management scholars that planning is a basic and pervasive function of management; differences which exist are semantic in nature.

Planning is concerned with the development of a plan; it involves mental activity and specifies what should be done, how it should be done, where action is effected, who is responsible, and why such action is necessary. It involves the selection of suitable alternatives for any activity. Planning involves the element of futurity with the degree of

futurity becoming greater as higher organizational levels are involved.
Henri Fayol called it "prevoyance" or "to foresee," and used the term in
the sense of both assessing the future and making provision for it. Several decades have passed since Fayol used it in this sense in an industrial complex. Military leaders had visualized "plans" and did "planning"
several centuries before Fayol's concept of the term. In the late 1870's
and 1880's many executives in Eastern manufacturing institutions concerned with metal working and the construction of machinery began to
evaluate production planning problems, especially in relation to standards and efficiency. These factors were generally identified as matters
which could be investigated in a scientific manner and planned so as to
optimize the resource employment available to the enterprise. Most planning in this respect was short range, as defined in this paper.

Frederick W. Taylor focused attention on planning when he described his planning room in his system of management. Some twenty-five
years after Taylor used the term the word was applied to the lay-out of
municipalities or other areas. City planning and regional planning are
definite and understandable uses of the term. Industrial planning,
military planning, and municipal planning remained dominant fields of
usage of the word until after the establishment of the Union of Socialist Soviet Republics and especially until the depression of 1929. Then
the terms "national planning" and "social-economic planning" came into
general use.[2]

---

[2]H. S. Person, "On Planning," The Society For The Advancement of
Management Journal (December, 1936), p. 143.

"Planning concepts" in the long-range sense existed in the military establishment long before the rise of the management profession; planning in the short-range sense envisioned in this paper existed both in the military and civilian organizations existing at the turn of the century. It only required the emergence and development of a management philosophy to give birth to long-range concepts within the industrial components of American business. However, American business appears to have had, around the turn of the present century, conceptualized short-range planning techniques. The economic and social forces in American business which facilitated the development of a concept and later philosophy of long-range planning is reflected in the writings of businessmen and scholars of that period.

Webster defines a concept as a mental image of a thing formed by a generalization from particulars; also as an idea of what a thing in general should be. One cannot believe that America's great industrialists, such as Allen, Frick, Ford, Patterson, Kettering, and many others, did not have a concept of long-range planning. Surely they must have had "images of the future" when they planned for future expansions, product development, capital acquisitions, and a myriad other considerations in their activities. Unfortunately, however, many of these industrial and business leaders failed to set down their images in the literature of the time and thus many of their concepts were lost to posterity. Fortunately, however, some educators and businessmen did commit their ideas to writing and it is these writings that make it possible to identify and trace the origin and development of a philosophy of long-range planning. Most of the writers were a product of their environment and accordingly wrote of local circumstances as they affected their organ-

izations. Only a few individuals in the early part of the twentieth century had the originality and foresight to conceptualize the abstractions
of the future position of their business. From these few writings one
can trace the evolving threads of thought concerning long-range planning
as it was contemplated in the first few decades of the present century.

The ensuing portions of this chapter will, therefore, be devoted
to tracing the developing philosophy of long-range planning as it was reflected in the literature of the time. The early literature was limited
and sketchy regarding the subject. Periodical literature, rather than
books, even in contemporary times, still reflects the preponderance of
thinking on long-range planning. The frequency of articles (either in
business periodicals or edited book collections) on long-range planning
is reflected in Table 1.[3] The number of articles by period is comprised
of articles or books either devoted in entirety to the subject of long-
range planning or which discusses the subject in some part or detail.
No differentiation is attempted between periodicals and books; furthermore, the articles and books reflected in the period prior to 1930 contain rather simplified references to the subject and do not attempt any
development of integrating factors, forces, and effects. Later writings
(1930-1961) show a progressive conceptualization of long-range planning
reflections. The majority of the literature has appeared in the last
decade. Thus it can be considered that the development of a philosophy
of long-range planning is a relatively recent phenomenon if the magnitude of literature appearing on the subject is the criterion. One must,
however, temper this observation with the thought that much of the thinking on long-range planning never manifested itself in the literature of

-----

[3]The indexes from which the articles on long-range planning were
taken are discussed on page 26.

the period but rather is reflected in the individual corporation files and is consequently unavailable to the general management profession.

TABLE 1

FREQUENCY OF ARTICLES AND BOOKS ON SUBJECT OF
LONG-RANGE PLANNING

Period	Number of Articles/Books Appearing During Period
1910 and prior periods	--
1910 - 1920	2
1920 - 1930	8
1930 - 1940	24
1940 - 1950	26
1950 - 1961	121
Total	181

Early Long-Range Planning Rudiments (1880 - 1900)

Any review of long-range planning rudiments must be made in the light of the industrial and economic climate of the period under consideration. In the United States the development of the factory system was hastened by the demands of the Civil War and in subsequent decades Americans occupied themselves increasingly with manufacturing. Until the decade of the eighties agriculture was the principal source of wealth, but the Census of 1890 showed that manufacturing had become of prime importance in terms of national wealth. Ten years later the value of manufactured products was more than double that of agriculture.[4] The accelerated development in manufacturing resulted from the demands of an extending and insatiable market. Increasing growth of the population required ever larger quantities of goods to meet needs. New demands developed and

[4]Twelfth Census of The United States, Vol. VII, Chapter 2.

as a result of these forces important new industries were created; a steady but slow improvement in the well-being of the population and a consequent increase in purchasing power was realized. Manufacturers were aided greatly by the abundance and richness of natural resources with the basic raw materials for practically every manufacturing industry to be found within the country.

Manufacturing showed a striking concentration, especially along certain lines, into a relatively smaller number of establishments and the economies of large scale production were vigorously pursued. Legislation was favorable to big business in the form of land grants, protective tariffs, a laissez-faire policy on the part of government, and the full protection of property rights under the Fifth and Fourteenth Amendments. In the seventies and eighties the trust movement and other forms of combination were attempted in order to consolidate greater industrial strength under a single management hierarchy. In the latter part of the Nineteenth century laissez-faire reached its peak and began to decline. Anti-trust legislation tempered the influence of the large corporations and competition became more vigorous and perhaps more fair.

By 1890 the United States had become a major manufacturing nation with the technological and distribution capability to produce goods at a relatively low cost. Favorable legislation and capital availability enabled the railroads to expand and extend markets to the western and southern parts of the country. Communication facilities, notably the telegraph system, fostered the further expansion of markets and sources of raw materials. The increasing size of industrial concerns, the ever-widening markets and lines of communications, and the growing complexity

of the large corporations stimulated the development of a business economy where more efficient management methods were required.

In the industrial and military preparations for the Spanish-American
War recognition was given to the role of pre-planning, especially typified
by the confusion and turmoil which resulted because no plans had been developed for the deployment of the nation's armed forces. In the military
establishment action was taken to develop a general staff capable of drawing up long-range plans. Little evidence exists, however, to indicate
that the Spanish-American War had any influence on industry in the development of long-range planning concepts other than to establish some rudimentary factors thereof. The combinations of Rockefeller, within his oil
enterprise; of the United States Steel Corporation, which brought under
one ownership and management ore mines, ships, railraods, blast furnaces,
rolling mills, and plants; and of the tobacco industry, where the growing,
curing, packaging, and distribution of the finished tobacco product was
integrated all give strong indication that some basic and "futurity" planning was effected. Whether this planning was done as an expedient of the
moment or was a deliberate and conscious long-term concept is difficult
to say. It should be recognized, however, that the basic rudiment of
long-range planning existed, probably for the first time, in American
business. The above combinations, to name just a few, where huge quantities of the factors of production of men, capital, and land were employed under a centralized form of management, created a peculiar situation which made imperative the appearance of basic long-range planning
techniques.

The management literature of this period is devoid of any specific
reference to a concept of long-range planning except management literature

associated with the military establishments. The rudiments of long-term
planning, however, did exist and were manifested in the actions of the
industrial and business combinations and mergers of the period.

Drury claimed, in 1915, that: "The roots of scientific management
are to be found in the life and thought of Frederick W. Taylor."[5] Taylor's pre-twentieth century contributions to the science of management
were centered around production techniques and did not contemplate the
administrative management problems of extra-organizational considerations
of the firm. His paper, "A Piece-Rate System," written in 1895, essentially was an explanation of his differential piece-rate scheme, and a
comparison of it with existing piece-rates, gain-sharing, and profit-
sharing schemes.[6] No management principles as such were given nor does
there appear to be any implicit or explicit reference to any long-term
considerations of the firm. Although the seeds of management thought
started to germinate during the last decade of the Nineteenth century
little periodical or book literature on the subject appeared. It remained for the environment and scholars of the Twentieth century to crys-
talize the evolving management thought. Within this period could be
found images of long-range planning.

---

[5]Horace B. Drury, Scientific Management A History And Criticism
(New York: Columbia University Press, 1915), p. 22.

[6]Frederick W. Taylor, "A Piece-Rate System," Transactions (American Society of Mechanical Engineers), XVI (1895), 856-58.

Evolution of Long-Range Planning Images (1900 - 1930)

Management thought changed significantly during the early part of
the Twentieth century. Management scholars, influenced by Taylor's
writings, paid more attention to the management problems at the shop
level and neglected somewhat the administrative or general management of
the enterprise. The rise of the corporate form of organization increased
the differentiation between ownership and management. Technology advanced rapidly during the period 1900 - 1930, aided by the necessities
of development of war production and the post-war boom in the United
States. Management scholars began to classify the profession and differentiated the organic functions of management. It was in this period
that time dimensions were first applied to industrial planning; also,
this period fostered the differentiation of the engineering and management professions.

Economic and Industrial Climate

The growing population of the United States increased significantly
during the period 1900 to 1930. Technological advances and increasing
consumer demand fostered expansion of business and industry. Basic industries expanded and new industries arose such as automobile and air
transportation which in turn created a different type of demand. Significant advances in the development of mass production techniques were
motivated by World War I. American business developed a high degree of
prosperity and optimism in the early and middle years of the twenties.
Agriculture as a national source of wealth declined more and more in
favor of the advancing manufacturing.

In spite of many favorable factors in the economic situation there was a cyclical trend downward in the late 1920's. What finally occurred was the most severe depression in the history of the United States; and it occurred in the main because of the exuberant excesses of an unrestrained stock market and real estate inflation, manipulation on a scale never before practical, and spiraled faster and faster by people who had let their avarice get the better of their common sense. Underdeveloped marketing methods, declining foreign investment, low farm prices, sticky consumer prices, the real estate inflation, and the substantial and growing concentration of profits in large corporations and of individual incomes in the upper income groups all caused the slow-down of consumer durables and residential construction. Business capital outlays stopped growing and began to decline. The stock market crash, coming in the midst of the unfavorable situation, accelerated sharply the economic disequilibrium which occurred late in 1929.

Pioneers in Long-Range Planning

Henri Fayol's observations on the principles of general management first appeared in French in 1916 and did not appear in an English version until about 1920. Fayol placed considerable emphasis on the managerial function of prevoyance or looking ahead. He considered the process of thinking out a plan and ensuring its success as one of the greatest satisfactions that an intelligent man could experience as well as a powerful stimulant of human endeavor. In describing the planning process Fayol said:

> The maxim, "Managing means looking ahead" gives some idea of the importance attached to planning in the business world, and it is true that if foresight is not the whole of management at least it is an essential part of it. To foresee, in this context, means

both to assess the future and make provision for it; that is, foreseeing is itself action already. Planning is manifested on a variety of occasions and in a variety of ways, its chief manifestation, apparent sign and most effective instrument being the plan of action. The plan of action is, at one and the same time, the result envisaged, the line of action to be followed, the stages to go through, and methods to use. It is a kind of future picture wherein proximate events are outlined with some distinctness, whilst remote events appear progressively less distinct, and it entails the running of the business as foreseen and provided against over a definite period.[7]

The difficulties of creating a good plan of action were recognized by Fayol, who considered the management function as playing a significant part in planning but also noted that the planning process calls into play every important department and function of the business. His general features of a good plan of action, viz., unity, continuity, flexibility, and precision are appropriate today several decades after his writings were first published. In spite of his formulation of some general principles for planning, Fayol recognized that much development in this managerial function needed to be pursued by stating:

> In each case, then, comparable elements and models must be sought in business practice, after the fashion of the architect with a building to construct. But the architect, better served than the manager, can call upon books, courses in architecture, whereas there are no books on plans of action, no lessons in foresight, for management theory has yet to be formulated.[8]

Fayol develops a concept of long-range planning in his writing relative to the drawing up of a plan of action in a large mining and metallurgical firm. The entire plan is contemplated as being made up of a series

[7]Henri Fayol, General and Industrial Management (London: Pitman, 1949), p. 43.

[8]Ibid., p. 45.

of forecasts or separate plans with yearly, ten-yearly, monthly, weekly, daily, long-term, and special forecasts. Provision is provided for the correlation of long-range and annual forecasts through the process of annual review of the forecasts so as to maintain unity of plan for each year. The comprehensiveness of his forecasting can be exemplified by a brief examination of the contents of such forecasts as reflected in Figure 1.

Special forecasts envisioned by Fayol were for activities which exceeded one or several of the ten-year forecasts. The integration of all the forecasts, yearly, ten-yearly, and special, constituted the firm's general plan; such a plan, in turn, after approval by the board of directors, served as the guide, directive, and law for the entire corporate staff.

Fayol is described by Koontz and O'Donnell as perhaps the real father of modern management theory.[9] Without question he had an extraordinary insight into the problems which beset business management even today. While Taylor was primarily concerned with shop management, Fayol directed his writings to an examination of the functions of the general administrative manager; the attention given to long-range planning, both in his writings and in his business practice seems to qualify him as the first real pioneer in the development and evolution of long-range planning images, later to be taken up by other management scholars and woven into the evolving philosophy of long-range planning.

_____

[9]Harold Koontz and Cyril O'Donnell, Principles of Management (New York: McGraw-Hill Book Company, Inc., 1959), p. 23.

Yearly and Ten-Yearly Forecasts

Technical Section
Mining Rights, Premises, Plant
Extraction, Manufacture, Output
New Workings, Improvements.
Maintenance of Plant and Buildings
Production Costs

Commercial Section
Sales Outlets
Marketable Goods
Agencies, Contracts
Customers, Importance, Credit Standing
Selling Price

Financial Section
Capital, Loans Deposits   Supplies in Hand
Circulating Assets   Finished Goods
Available Assets   Debtors
    Liquid Assets

Reserves and Sundry Appropriation
Creditors   Wages
    Suppliers
    Sundry

Sinking Funds
Dividends
Bankers

Accounting
Balance Sheet
Profit and Loss Account
Statistics

Security
Accident Precautions
Works Police, Claims, Health Service
Insurance

Management
Plan of Action   Organization of Personnel Selection
Command   Coordination, Conferences
Control

Figure 1. Contents of forecasts as envisioned by Henri Fayol, as reflected in General and Industrial Management (London: Pitman, 1949),
p. 47.

Gantt makes an implicit reference to the long-term responsibilities of business and industrial leaders by recognizing that the maintenance of our civilization is dependent upon the service it gets from the industrial and business system. Economic catastrophe can be staved off, according to Gantt, ". . . if those in control of industry will recognize the seriousness of the situation and promptly present a positive program which definitely recognizes the responsibility of the industrial and business system to render such service as the community needs."[10] Whether Gantt had a premonition of the coming depression of 1929 - 1933 is not known; however, present day management theory does recognize that service can better be provided through the utilization of comprehensive planning techniques employed within a philosophy of management.

Gilbreth, writing on the science in management, recognized that management was already equipped in 1922 to apply a plan for the development of an industry or an organization. He stipulated that the early recognition of the trend, the laying out of the necessary plan is not work for untrained, inexperienced executives, but rather requires the trained thinker and installer to use the existing information for the betterment of the plant. While he gives credit for some plants having developed to such a stage that experts are at work making surveys, organizing, and forecasting the trend of future development, the majority of plants are as yet in an earlier stage where the chief necessities are to arouse interest in progress in the plant towards better management. Gilbreth, in further discussions, cites the example of long-term planning on the

---

[10]H. L. Gantt, Organizing For Work (New York: Harcourt, Brace & Howe, 1919), p. 153.

part of a great western university which, through a comprehensive process,
outlined its present and future requirements far ahead of the existing
needs. In writing of the success Gilbreth said:

> Not only has such development as has taken place in the twenty
> years since then followed the lines wisely laid down at that time,
> but undoubtedly much has found its way into the resources of the
> university, because those who had things to contribute knew that
> what they gave would be utilized in a directed, orderly fashion.
> As a result, these plans have served as a stimulus, as well as a
> conserving and guiding force, and have probably exceeded even the
> usefulness that their donor expected of them.[11]

Other rudiments of long-range planning appeared in literature during the early twenties. Oliver Sheldon, while recognizing the value of
planning to the business concern, cautioned that our progress in this respect would not lead us to any Utopia:

> He who sets himself either to design a future form of industry
> or to conjure up a vision of what industry may yet become, faces
> a problem not of logical construction or of scientific planning,
> but of continual adjustment and adaptation to circumstances which
> cannot be foretold. The value of such schemes is rather that
> they may trace the outline of our ideals, and thus mayhap can
> guide our progress. But that our progress will lead us to any
> prefigured land of promise is as improbable as the existence of
> Utopia itself.[12]

Sheldon further hints at long-range planning responsibilities when
he alludes to the intertwining of the individual as a worker and as a
social unit:

> It is impossible to disassociate life outside from life inside
> the factory. The one reacts upon the other because the indivi-

---

[11]Frank B. Gilbreth, Science In Management For The One Best Way
To Do Work (Milan: Societa Umanitaria, 1922), p.

[12]Oliver Sheldon, The Philosophy of Management (London: Sir Isaac
Pitman & Sons, Ltd., 1923), p. 280.

dual entity remains constant. Management inevitably, therefore, is loaded with responsibilities which stretch beyond the local sphere of production.[13]

Webster Robinson proposed to show that "regardless of the size or character of a business there are certain basic factors and relationships which are essential for its organization."[14] In this respect he placed considerable emphasis on the basic purpose or objective of a business being expressed in a general policy which gives a definite outline of future plans for the enterprise. Success, according to Robinson, is achieved by planning ahead to include the creation of serviceable plans made within the framework of the basic purpose of the business. Forecasting was visualized as a subfunction of control; "Control," noted Robinson, ". . . involves three principal elements: forecasting of results; recording of results; and placement of responsibility for results. A retrospective system of control, from which all forecasting or planning is absent, is of little value."[15] Although Robinson attempted to formulate principles of organization and reduce them to a few fundamentals that an executive should recognize and consider in constructing his organization he alluded to a few basic considerations of planning which extended beyond the immediate future of the business.

Psychology had its influence on the growing management thought of the twenties. Leadership, in its intellectual aspect, was described by

---

[13]Ibid., p. 82.

[14]Webster Robinson, Fundamentals of Business Organization (New York: McGraw-Hill Book Co., 1925), p. vii.

[15]Ibid., pp. 147-148.

Metcalf as an ability to define ultimate and immediate objectives or
". . . what is to be accomplished tomorrow. Leadership in industry, no
less than in war, involves both strategy and tactics. Purposes remote
and immediate must be formulated, and the best means of realizing them
thought out."[16] Metcalf goes further in describing the attributes of
leadership by stating that success is not attained, regardless of the
personal qualities of the leader, unless goals are established, means
for attaining them clearly thought out, the plans are definitely laid
out and put into the proper form for easy understanding on the part of
those responsible for carrying them out. Leadership that is something
less than the foregoing can achieve relative success, says Metcalf, if
somewhere within the organizational hierarchy there exists a superior adviser or a capable planning department to perform the planning for the
leader. But, according to Metcalf, "Planning and intellectual foresight
are unquestionably basic to effective leadership."[17]

Industry leaders began thinking and writing about business planning during the twenties. Vice-president Donaldson Brown of the General
Motors Corporation cited intelligent forecasting and planning as the
mechanism necessary to mitigate the adverse effects of the business cycle.
In describing the methodology that General Motors uses in forecasting consumer demand as a basis for effecting long-term planning two fundamentals
of planning were conceived: (1) statistical, ascertaining the statistical
facts bearing upon consumer demand and (2) constructive, or the efforts
toward improving probability both in long-term and short-term time ele-

---

[16]Henry C. Metcalf, The Psychological Foundations of Management
(New York: A. W. Shaw Company, 1927), p. 247.

[17]Ibid., p. 249.

ments. Such influences as consumer appeal in style, functioning, and ser-
viceability, were given consideration in General Motors Corporation's near
and far term planning processes. Brown further believed that business
planning could do much to stabilize business conditions.[18] The pervasive-
ness of the planning function was recognized by Brown as "Forecasting and
planning is the essence of modern-day business management. It is not the
function of an individual or a department -- it is the conscious, coopera-
tive work of an organization."[19]

The period 1900-1930 provided ample opportunity in terms of the
economic environment for the evolution of long-range planning images.
Early appearances and the influence such writings had on the thinking of
management students may be summarized as indicated below.

Summary of the Contributions of the Period

1. Fayol undoubtedly contributed the first and most fundamental
thinking and writing on long-range planning in the business world. His
recognition of the importance of a business's future and his forecasting
techniques were extraordinary contributions for his time. Credit must be
given to Fayol for perhaps the first functionally integrated image of
long-range planning policy, procedures, and techniques.

[18]Donaldson Brown, "Forecasting and Planning Vital To Industrial
Prosperity; Method of General Motors Corporation," Iron Age (May 10, 1928),
pp. 1321-1322.

[19]Donaldson Brown, "Forecasting and Planning as a Factor in Stabilizing Industry," Sales Management (January 26-February 2, 1929), p.
258-259.

2. The preponderance of literature on planning which appeared during this period was concerned with short-range planning, that was production oriented, and did not contemplate extra-organizational considerations.

3. An attempt was made by several writers to show a relationship between the organizational service objective of a business and its future, implying thereby that some type of long-term planning would stabilize business, consequently contributing to a greater sense of social and service responsibility on the part of executive management.

4. The existence of a requirement for long-range planning was recognized at least as a rudiment; however, little attempt was made to pursue a solution to develop long-term planning techniques and processes. Some writers, in recognizing the future of a business, suggested that planning for an organization's future could be improved by studying other company's methods.

5. Forecasting and futurity planning, as a functional area of effort in a business unit, were used somewhat synonymously; planning was conceived of as an organic function but received relatively little attention in the development of time dimensions thereof.

6. Psychology pointed up a relationship between leadership and planning with the latter being a fundamental attribute of a successful leader. Industry leaders, doubtlessly influenced by the scientific management movement, began developing rudimentary forecasting techniques, analyzed consumer demand, and used these tools to assist in some elementary long-range planning. The automotive industry appears to have led the way in this respect.

7. Long-range planning, as a fairly well differentiated function of management, existed in mental images as a business necessity, as a

stabilizer of industry, and as an attribute of leadership. While Fayol,
in 1916, pointed the way for an integrated approach to such planning,
American business failed to develop any real appreciation for the philosophical possibilities of such a technique. It would take the conse-
quences of the great depression to motivate business leaders into seeking a solution to the long-term future stability of their organization.

Recognition of the Need for Long-Range Planning in
American Business (1930-1940)

The most significant economic event of the 1930's was the continued depression that had struck the American nation in 1929. The previous decade had fostered a high degree of growth and prosperity in business
and industry and there was little concern to the future except to relate
it to an even greater opulence. From the period 1930-1940 unemployment
approximated twenty-five per cent of the nation's civilian labor force;
failure of business became commonplace and according to Mee, "Businessmen lost prestige as well as the confidence of the public."[20]

Economic and Industrial Climate

Corporate and personal income declined in this period; consumer
demand fell off sharply; and industry and business became concerned with
cost reduction and immediate problems. Little concern was given to long-
run considerations of the firm inasmuch as mere survival became a primary problem for many businesses. Scholars of the period began to search
for an economic organization and philosophy that would provide more stability than the existing tempered laissez-faire of the Republican adminis-

---

[20]John Franklin Mee, A History of Twentieth Century Management
Thought (The Ohio State University, 1959, doctoral dissertation), p. 200.

tration. By 1932 the volume of United States industry had been reduced
to about one-half of the 1929 volume. The market economy, established
since 1900, had collapsed.[21] Unions, given sanction by society and recognition by the NRA and the Wagner Act, fostered collective bargaining as
a way of life for industrial relations. During the 1930's the labor
unions increased membership from 3.6 million to 8.9 million.[22] In the
latter period of the decade American business became concerned about the
preparation for involvement in the European war. The proposed lend-lease
program of the Democratic administration promised to provide a stimulus
to American business and industry. An economic change, perhaps for the
better, was in the making.

Management as a profession became recognized by scholars in the
writing of the period. H. W. Prentis, Jr., in describing this new type
of management person said:

> I refer to what are commonly known as 'career' men in business:
> men who never hope to own any large portion of the enterprise of
> which they are a part; men who realize that the bonanza days of
> the old captains of industry are over; men who see in business
> something more than the mere making of money; men who are imbued
> with a deep sense of social stewardship; men who are keenly sen-
> sible of the fact that they are trustees of other people's money
> with heavy responsibilities to discharge to employees and the
> public as well as to the stockholders; men who find deep spirit-
> ual satisfaction in the direction of their brains and energy to-
> ward the creation of a better and more abundant life for all of
> their fellow human beings.[23]

Government entered into a greater period of business involvement
than had appeared on the American scene heretofore. The economic catas-

---

[21]Ibid.

[22]Gordon F. Bloom and Herbert R. Northrup, Economics of Labor Relations (Homewood, Illinois: Richard D. Irwin, Inc., 1961), p. 82.

[23]H. W. Prentis, Jr., "Liberal Education for Business and Industry,"
Bulletin of the American Association of University Professors (Autumn,
1952), p. 346.

trophe of the thirties stimulated industry and government leaders to develop a philosophy of management which would reduce the probability of
another depression. Over-production, excess capacity, satiated demand,
union influence, and the increasing role of government presented short
and long-run considerations in developing and managing the business organization. Thus in the 1930's the stage was set for the realization,
on the part of business and industry leaders, that the management function of an organization had to contemplate factors, forces, and effects
well beyond the local time and the existing environment.

Contributions to Long-Range Planning Thought

Dennison's book on Organization Engineering was designed to identify and present a solution to the problems concerned with making a success of group activity. While he recognized that "not many tasks can
be planned in full detail for years ahead,"[24] full credit was given to
the necessity for the organization to look ahead but in so doing it must
recognize the limitations which restrict its ability to consider and
visualize the future. Dennison was influenced by the military concept
of planning as well as the probability of recurring business recessions:

> It is the custom of general staffs of armies to study in advance
> with considerable care what it would be necessary and effective
> to do in case this or that contingency should happen. There are
> many occasions upon which this is a wise policy for the general
> staffs of many other kinds of organizations to follow. For ex-
> ample, at any time during periods of business prosperity it is
> likely that a period of recession is ahead - at least this has
> always been true in the past. The exact nature of the period
> can seldom be foreseen, and specific provisions to meet it can-

---

[24]Henry Dennison, Organization Engineering (New York: McGraw-
Hill Book Co., Inc., 1931), pp. 149-150.

not be worked out in detail, but general provisions can be; and in any case it can be arranged that such a period will not catch an organization wholly surprised and mentally unprepared.[25]

Dennison's main contributions to long-range planning are (1) recognition of the role that the general staff agencies in the military organizations have played in planning and (2) the possibility that such a "general staff" approach can be used by business and industry to prepare better for future operations, particularly the best course of action to prescribe for business recessions. In further discussing the role of planning in the business organization Dennison, in speaking of the decentralization ramifications of planning, stated that

> . . . Authority is in essence the working out of plans which meet conditions and are understandable by those they effect. Hence, as much in the field as at the center the planner must have a knowledge of objectives, conditions, and personnel. Authority in both cases goes with knowledge and ability. A chief difference lies in the span of time and the variety of conditions and personnel to be covered by the planning. The time span to be covered by central management may run into years, while at the edges of the field, planning may have to run merely from day to day.[26]

Although Dennison's main interest was in organizing and leadership, with relatively little consideration being given to the organic functions of planning and control, his perspective of the long-run considerations of the firm represents a contribution to the evolving recognition of the need for long-range planning.

The period of the thirties might be characterized as an era of planning proposals. In the previous decade most planning was reflected in the form of discussion and research in city and regional planning

---

[25]Ibid., p. 151.

[26]Ibid., p. 159.

while the Federal Reserve System, the Federal Trade Commission, and the
Bureau of Foreign and Domestic Commerce assumed a stronger position in
business. The panic of 1929 and the following depression precipitated a
strong economic planning movement in the United States. In the period
shortly after the start of the depression economic planning had become
almost a popular craze. Socialists, liberals, and business men joined in
the movement. A committee of the Chamber of Commerce of the United States
of America developed a plan for stabilizing employment; the Swope Plan
contemplated a system of self regulation of business; scholars such as
W. B. Donham, Dean of the Harvard Business School, called on businessmen to develop business planning with consideration to the social relations and functions of business. On the other hand, socialists and re-
forms of the more radical type proposed overall national planning and
controls somewhat similar to that which existed in Soviet Russia at that
time.[27] Without doubt Russia's national economic planning manifested in
the form of a series of five-year plans had an influence on economists,
politicians, and business leaders in the United States. Some of the
other plans that were put forth in the early thirties were these:

1. Stuart Chase proposed a ten-year plan for economic stabilization and included in it the recreating of the War Industries Board into
a Peace Industries Board.

2. Charles A. Beard proposed a National Economic Council as the
center of his economic plan and a Board of Strategy and Planning to develop and implement national economic plans.

_____

[27]Henrietta M. Larson, Guide To Business History (Cambridge: Harvard University Press, 1948), pp. 942-943.

3. Matthew Wall, of the AFL, called for an American Congress of
Industry to formulate a ten-year economic plan.[28]

A few scholars and businessmen developed a counter movement to the
social-economic planning idea, viz., that business planning, done individually, would in the aggregate provide high production and contribute to
the general social security and well-being of the society more than would
a strong form of centralized government planning. Traditional planning
by business units, perhaps augmented by a development of group planning,
but yet as a primary individual business responsibility, began to be advocated as an alternative to some type of socialist state planning.[29] At
the time, Warren Bishop, Managing Editor of Nation's Business, offered a
plea for individual business planning by stating, "If we are to have a
plan for business it ought to be a plan by business."[30]

National leaders of the day began to advocate some type of social
planning, not only as a solution to the business depression, but also to
reduce some of the waste and haphazardness of the economic system.
Roosevelt, writing in 1933, said:

> We cannot review carefully the history of our industrial advance
> without being struck by its haphazardness, with the gigantic waste
> with which it has been accomplished - with the superfluous dupli-
> cation of productive facilities, the continual scrapping of still
> useful equipment, the tremendous mortality in industrial and com-
> mercial undertakings, the thousands of dead-end trails in which
> enterprise has been lured, the profligate waste of natural re-
> sources. Much of this waste is the inevitable by-product of pro-

---

[28]Warren Bishop, "Rain of Plans," Nation's Business (August, 1931).

[29]Larson, op. cit., p. 943.

[30]Bishop, op. cit., p. 36.

gress in a society which values individual endeavor and which is
susceptible to the changing tastes and customs of the people of
which it is composed. But much of it, I believe, could have been
prevented by greater foresight and by a larger measure of social
planning.[31]

While some recognition was given to the role of social planning, that in-

cluded a type of state-controlled business planning, other leaders of the

day were frankly skeptical of the then ability of business to conduct long-

term planning. Keynes, the English economist, noted:

> If we speak frankly, we have to admit that our basis of knowledge
> for estimating the yield ten years hence of a railway, a copper
> mine, a textile factory, and good will of a patent medicine, an
> Atlantic liner, a building in the city of London amounts to lit-
> tle and sometimes to nothing.[32]

Other economists of the period supported the idea of developing some sort

of socio-economic planning system for the nation. While business contin-

ued to support the idea of individual business planning as a partial pana-

cea for the nation's difficulties, the influence of the social planners

was manifested in the welfare and social nature of the first few years of

New Deal legislation. Some economists and socialists attributed the de-

pression to the unplanned character of our economic system. While Clark

recognized the value of some form of social control of business, he gave

due credit to the concept that planning was no easy panacea but that it

could make real contributions to the present stage of industrial develop-

ment in the United States. According to Clark,

> Planning is no easy panacea; that much is clearly evident. It can
> easily make serious mistakes. But it contains possibilities of real
> contributions to our present stage of industrial development. And

---

[31]Franklin D. Roosevelt, Looking Forward (The John Day Company,
1933), pp. 43-44.

[32]John Maynard Keynes, The General Theory of Employment, Interest,
and Money (London: Harcourt, Brace and Company, Inc., 1936), pp. 149-150.

an economic system in as serious a state as our own cannot afford
not to explore and develop these possibilities to the utmost.[33]

The approach of most economists during this period undoubtedly was influenced by their classical economic education, i.e., the average economist probably was skeptical about any sort of grand and all encompassing
national planning. Economic theory had been built on the assumption
that the business world was made up chiefly of a very large number of
independent, competitive units. The failure of the then existing economic order, however, cast serious doubts on the concept of laissez-faire
in our society and thus some economists appeared to be swayed in favor
of some sort of planning under a socialist order.

It was during this period that trade associations began to be considered as a strong influence in effecting business planning, especially
in the long-term sense. The U. S. Chamber of Commerce, through its Committees on Continuity of Business and Employment, suggested in 1931 that
a National Economic Council be developed as an advisory board on such
economic problems as ways and means of controlling and directing production; trade associations were to provide the leadership for this activity,
viz.,

> Individual planning in every industry where such planning is pos-
> sible was the Committee's final recommendation as to long-term
> remedies. Much can be accomplished, it was suggested, toward
> preventing or mitigating the effects of seasonal depressions
> through adaption of company planning methods. Leadership in
> this movement, the Committee declared, rests with trade asso-
> ciations.[34]

---

[33]John M. Clark, Social Control of Business (New York: McGraw-Hill
Book Company, Inc., 1939), p. 471.

[34]"Planning Business Stability," Nation's Business (November, 1931),
pp. 56-58.

Pinchbeck, writing in Domestic Engineering in 1931, criticized the lack
of planning in the American business and economic system. America, he
said, ". . . has grown up on an economic philosophy of individualism."[35]
He further advocated the use of trade associations to sophisticate the
business planning that would provide stability in the economy.

The depression hit the existing trade associations hard and caused
a shift from the concept of the trade association as a price-protection
agency to that of a planning board for its industry. These associations
advocated the shift of scientific management from the individual firm to
the industry. Planning, in the efficient company, was visualized as encompassing not only the individual business and its future, but the industry as well. Planning, was conceived as a shift from guesswork for the
immediate future to a systematic search on the business's future as far
as possible over a series of years. It was recognized that a need existed for business to have a planning department to do business projections over the next few years. Short-term sales and financial budgets
were to be supplemented with a long-term budget for the industry as well
as the company. Heermance, speaking before a session on long-term planning held at the annual meeting of the American Society of Mechanical
Engineers, New York, New York, December 5-9, 1932, said, "The members of
the trade associations must be trained in long-range planning and given
the necessary tools."[36] Planning was conceived of by Heermance as an-

---

[35]R. B. Pinchbeck, "Planning is a Big Problem of Business,"
Domestic Engineering (September 19, 1931), p. 91.

[36]E. L. Heermance, "Trade Association's Part in Coordinate Planning," Mechanical Engineering (February, 1933), p. 103.

other name for good business management. With regard to national planning
he said:

> The progress of scientific management will be from the company
> to the industry, from the industry to the nation, from the na-
> tion to the business world. We are now entering on the second
> of these four stages. Until industry planning has made con-
> siderable headway, national planning must wait.37

Meermance's writing has another significance besides that reported, viz.,
it was a condensation of an address he delivered at a session on long-
term planning held at the annual meeting of the American Society of Mechanical Engineers, under the auspices of the Management Division. The
meeting was held during the period of December 5 through 9, 1932. Based
upon the author's research for this dissertation this appeared as the
first evidence of any meeting of a professional association which had a
session devoted to the subject of long-range planning.38 Other professional organizations devoted time to a discussion of the broad subject
of business planning not only for operations within a single plant or a
single industry but also in the broader field of national and international economics. Major Lynn Urwick, Director of The International
Management Institute, advocated an international planning department
properly equipped to effect scientific planning, "organized, not along
national lines emphasizing national differences, but industry by industry and function by function. Picture it as a clearing house of statistics of vital importance to business."39 R. J. McFall, Chief Stat-

---

37Ibid., p. 104.

38An attempt was made to obtain a copy of the minutes of this meeting from the American Society of Mechanical Engineers, 345 E. 47th St.,
New York, 17, N.Y. However, that organization, while it had knowledge of
the meeting, did not know of the existence of any of the minutes thereof.

39"Broad Aspects of Industrial Planning Discussed By Taylor Society,"
Iron Age (May 7, 1931), p. 1534.

istician for Distribution, Bureau of the Census, Department of Commerce, in discussing the possibilities of business planning, particularly in the long-term sense, pointed out the need for more statistical knowledge of distribution in order to predict the general buying power of the public. With regard to the possibility of business planning contributing to the stabilization of industry he noted:

> Stabilization of any industry can only be effected by considering industrial and economic conditions throughout the country as well as the distribution of the products of the particular industry involved.[40]

McFall recognized the importance of the external economy to a company's planning.

Other government officials played a significant part in developing a need on the part of businessmen for a long-term planning capability. Frederick M. Feiker, Director of the Department of Commerce's Bureau of Foreign and Domestic Commerce, supported the idea that national economic planning had no place in America; that it must, instead, rest upon the intelligence and ingenuity of the individual manufacturers. He suggested an approach to maintain a continuous adjustment of production facilities to market demands by carefully forecasting of sales one year ahead and three to ten years ahead as far as investment policy was concerned. The true aim of business economic planning, he believed, provided for--

1. Market research and analysis, determining the most probable long-term market growth factor for each principal product.

---

[40]Ibid., p. 1533.

2. Product research to determine the optimum product.

3. An investment and equipment replacement program.[41]

The growing literature on the subject of long-term planning was not without contribution from high-ranking industry leaders. R. Eide, President of the Ohio Bell Telephone Company, in describing the role of commercial research in his company, conceived of it as the function of taking known facts, trends, and tendencies of the past and from them building and planning the business of the next year, five years, ten years, or even twenty-five or fifty years hence. Planning was conceived of as an activity requiring a search of the lessons of experience and then adjusting these lessons in light of the present and probable conditions of the company.[42] He recognized the dynamic nature of the economic structure of the American economy when he stated:

> To continue making a profit a business must see ahead, not merely guess ahead; it must program its future under carefully prepared plans, and it must be alert at all times to change its future program with each new set of conditions. So far as humanly possible, it must anticipate what will happen and what is required.[43]

The newsprint industry expressed an appreciation for long-range planning early in the thirties. S. T. Frame pointed out that the newsprint industry, afflicted with excessive difficulties because of the depression and over capacity, could get out of its difficulties only by

---

[41]F. M. Feiker, "Sensible Economic Planning," Printers Ink (March 3, 1932), pp. 71-72.

[42]R. Eide, "Planning Ahead - The Place of Commercial Research," Special Libraries (July, 1931), pp. 240-246.

[43]Ibid., p. 240.

". . . long-range planning rather than in terms of makeshift measures ar
rived at for immediate solution of the major troubles."[44] In reporting

on a survey of industry Frame reported favorable fundamental conditions

existing for the future planning of newsprint. He identified some broad

steps for effecting long-range planning: (1) Long-range planning for

capacity, raw materials, and "policy," and (2) long-range planning in

budgets, cost, and financial matters.[45] The significance of his writ-

ings rests in the fact that what he advocated had application not only

to the newsprint industry but to some of the fundamentals of long-range

planning (to be developed later in this paper). In a later article Frame

offers further information on the procedures the newsprint industry used

to predict newsprint consumption and then to make long-range predictions.

Problems of estimating future consumption are evaluated, particularly

two general elements involved in the estimate of the future trend, viz.,

population and the average annual amount of newsprint purchased by each

individual citizen. As a result of the long-range study of the industry

several requirements of the industry were summarized.

1. Capacity must be scaled down to consumptive requirements.

2. Operations should be concentrated in low-cost mills.

3. Inefficient mills should be permanently closed down.[46]

---

[44]S. T. Frame, "Planning for the Future of News Print," Paper
Trade Journal (April 28, 1932), p. 18.

[45]Ibid., p. 18-20.

[46]S. T. Frame, "Planning for the News Print Industry," Harvard
Business Review (July, 1932), pp. 441-452.

Other literature of the period expressed a concern with the long-term considerations of the individual business unit. While these writings did not develop any integrated approach to the solution of long-term problems, they are important because they add to the growing recognition of a long-run concept of business operation. These articles are briefly summarized below:

1. "Policies must be developed for the long-run for creating a plan which contemplates short-run and long-run considerations."[47]

2. "To get on to a sound basis, so that in the future we will avoid a repetition of the past war excesses, we must do more planning and less executing."[48]

3. N. B. Hinson, Chief Engineer of The Southern California Edison Company, Ltd., reported the use of a System Planning Committee to do long-range planning to meet the increasing requirements for more electrical power. The building for growth within the company started with the coordinated planning within the utility, i.e., with the operating departments, engineering, sales, and others participating. Plans for future growth and requirements were based primarily on the estimated number of people to be served and their economic and social characteristics. Recognition was given to the great difficulty in anticipating the economic trend over future years.[49]

---

[47] W. J. Donald, "Forget Your Jitters - And Have A Plan," Forbes (March 15, 1933), p. 8.

[48] D. F. Kettering, "Today's Need - More Planning and Less Executing," Iron Age (May 11, 1933), p. 733.

[49] "Building For Growth," Electrical World (May 22, 1937), pp. 79-84.

4. "Those enterprises, on the other hand, which are operated by management whose viewpoints cover a longer period . . . who are willing to advertise today to build stability for tomorrow, who prepare their business levees for a future flood; those concerns take the valleys, peaks, and the inclined planes over the years in the same strong, powerful stride."[50]

5. "The depression years prevented many business leaders from giving sufficient time to long-range planning because the problem of maintaining the mere integrity of the business demanded the full time of the executive personnel. Profit is recognized as a concept which envisions a long-pull where progress is slow."[51]

The urgencies of the immediate situation in the depressed 30's forced business to resort to expediency instead of planned policies. In some cases valuable plans that had been thought out in the previous periods of prosperity were abandoned because of sheer impatience, executive caprice, vagary, or prejudice. Failure to have a "Future Demands" department charged with the responsibility of looking ahead forced many concerns to neglect the future altogether, for existing management was preoccupied with immediate operating problems, especially with gaining a quick profit without serious concern for the future. E. H. Schell suggested the need for "thoughtful progressiveness based on long-term trends of certainty." In describing American industry Schell further

---

[50]R. A. Foulice, "Prepare Your Business For Tomorrow," _Dun's Review_ (April, 1937), pp. 47-48.

[51]"Day to Day vs Long Pull Planning For Business Profits," _American Business Combined With System_ (November, 1938), p. 25.

noted that a change had occurred; "for the first time in more than a decade, a distinct massing of the sentiment among business leaders appeared that dictates that the United States must, in the future, be able to move forward with a greater degree of certainty."[52] He visualized that business policies could no longer be built upon the shifting sands of day-to-day expediency, but that business leaders had to view the future deliberately, and with a greater exercise of forethought. Present trends, he said, contain elements of future certainty. Industry was conceived of as requiring long-term foresight in order to --

1. Accumulate financial and executive reserve for the future.

2. Meet a new position of social responsibility.

3. Meet increasing competition, both from within an industry and from new products developed outside of the then existing industry.

4. Take into consideration in the business posture the increasing emphasis on industry-community relationships; the swing of consumer interest to more objective qualities; and the influence of human relations.[53] Schell summarized his concept of future planning by stating: "Expediency in business policy is to be replaced by a more deliberate and thoughtful progressiveness, based upon the long-term trends of certainty."[54]

One of the most significant writings of the technique of planning was offered by H. S. Person who differentiated between the planning that takes place in an individual mind which is limited to the abilities, range of influence, and facilities of the individual executive, and the

---

[52]E. H. Schell, "Training Men to Look Ahead," Nation's Business (March, 1940), p. 30.

[53]Ibid., pp. 128-129.   [54]Ibid., p. 29.

planning that is effected through the development of an <u>institutional</u> <u>mind</u> in the organization. The <u>institutional</u> <u>mind</u> is independent of individuals who come and go and possesses its institutional power of perception (research), memory (records), capacity for reasoning (group analysis), and power to direct the application of conclusions through a period longer than the life of an individual (industrial administration). Person gives due credit to the planning abilities of such individuals as Marshall Field, John D. Rockefeller, and Andrew Carnegie, but indicates that these individuals set about the development within their enterprises of a technique of employment and planning by an institutional mind as indicated above.[55] In regard to industry's contribution to socio-economic planning Person said:

> Planning, in this technical meaning of the term as understood by large-scale engineering and industry, has not yet been adapted to the social purposes of government in the United States. In the common meaning of the term, individual leaders and individual administrations have had their individual plans, but these have pivoted on individuals and have been transitory. A continuing institutional mind, especially charged with the responsibility of formulating some comprehensive long-run social plan, has never been established. However, the complications and confusion of our cultural and economic life are becoming such that the planning of a better adjustment of life to environment, and of cultural and economic institutions to each other, appears essential. The technique of such planning cannot make a better beginning than to adapt the technique developed by engineering and industry.[56]

Person's contribution to the developing framework of long-range planning concepts is an implied one, viz., that the large institutions of the period had developed a type of institutional mind for planning of short-run operations; great individuals in industry had developed some form

---

[55]H. S. Person, "On the Technique of Planning," <u>Bulletin of the Taylor Society and of the Society of Industrial Engineers</u> (November, 1934), p. 29.

[56]<u>Ibid</u>., p. 31.

of long-range planning which, unfortunately, ceased to exist when that extraordinary individual passed from the scene. What is needed, implied Person, is an _institutional_ _mind_ which can conceive and perpetuate some form of _long-run_ _plan_ for the organization.

Summary of the General Contributions of the 1930-1940 Period

1. In the first half of the 1930's, the literature on long-range planning was concerned in the main with national or economic-social planning. Depressed conditions in the national economy caused social, political, and economic leaders to seek a panacea for the prostrate economy. A series of plans was suggested, many of which were tailored along the Russian five-year plans.

2. Although businessmen appeared to lose prestige in the public eye, the "career man" in business management arose as a product of the increased size and complexity of business organizations.

3. Scholars of the period began to speak of the long-term responsibilities of business leaders; the military planning staff, as a method of organization to consider and plan for the future, was studied and recommended for industry and business.

4. The immediate problem of survival in the depressed market conditions stifled the attention of business leaders to any serious concern about the long-run considerations of the future; however, businessmen in general became concerned about the popular support that social-economic planning on a national scale was receiving and offered individual business planning as an alternative to national economic planning.

5. Trade associations began to be considered as a possible strong influence in effecting business long-run planning on both an individual

business and on an industry scale. A professional association gave unusual attention to long-run planning for the time period involved and
held a session entirely devoted to the subject.

6. Industry leaders began to unite and tell of individual company planning techniques for long-term considerations. These leaders,
in the main, recognized the need for long-range planning but failed to
develop any integrated functional approach to the task. Planning for
long term was conceived of as a fundamental policy; techniques, procedures, and development of methodology to accomplish the long-term policy
was not conceptualized.

7. Politicians, business leaders, economists, and industrialists
recognized the need for long-range planning as a possible counter force
to the recessions and depressions which had plagued the national economy.
Long-range planning, as a differentiated functional area of organized
business effort, was conceptualized only in the individual minds of the
corporate management. The conceptualization of a long-range planning
approach in the "institutional mind" of the organized effort would wait
until a later period.

The Expansion of Long-Range Planning Concepts (1940-1950)
Industrial and Economic Climate

The industrial and economic climate of the forties was significantly influenced by World War #II. Preparation and conduct of a global
war called for unprecedented industrial and military expansion and cooperation. In the main, all economic activity was subordinated to the
necessity of waging a war; consumer products were in short supply and
the buying public postponed much of its normal consumption until the ter-
mination of hostilities. Unions gained in membership in the middle and

latter part of the decade and fostered a series of strikes that resulted
in marked gains in fringe and wage benefits expressed in long-term contracts. The period after World War II presented a unique opportunity for
the conversion of war plants to civilian production; excess capacity resulted in some industries as a consequence of the unrestrained expansion
during wartime. The time was opportune for the further expansion of some
long-range planning concepts that had been given fundamental development
in the preceding decade. Postwar planning became a grave concern for
many industries during the early forties; pent-up consumer demand presented a unique opportunity for product research and development. During
the period the cost of research and development increased significantly
and business slowly came to the realization that more planning for long-
term markets was required. Increasing research and development costs,
the increased complexity of individual businesses, the trend toward more
diversification, and the long-range effects of present day management decisions motivated management to investigate and expand the existing concepts of long-range planning.

Contributions from Literature

A significant study was conducted by Holden in 1941 on the planning
and control techniques of some selected companies in California. This
study indicated that the successful experience which many of the companies had, and the value they derived from long-range planning, suggested
a wider adoption of the practice by other companies. Lack of adequate
long-range planning was frequently caused by top management becoming preoccupied with daily operational matters, thereby neglecting the future

needs of the business. As regards the establishment of objectives, and

the compatibility of such objectives with short-range planning, Holden

said:

> Two of the companies which have outstanding plans of management
> establish their objectives five years ahead. Such long-term ob-
> jectives are necessarily tentative, subject to modification as
> time and circumstances require, but they are invaluable as guide-
> posts to assure the proper orientation, consistency, and reason-
> ableness of the definite near-term planning.[57]

The significance of this study is represented by the fact that an attempt

was made to evaluate the long-range planning experience of a company. Al-

though this was not the main purpose for conducting the study, it did pro-

vide some evidence of long-range planning practices.

Other long-range planning considerations were reflected in the lit-

erature of the period; in some cases by explicit reference and in others

by implication. Such an implication was contained in Stuart Chase's

treatise on the social responsibilities of business. Chase visualized

that management had to provide certain things to the society if any con-

tribution was to be made by business to an improved standard of living.

These objectives he conceived of as:

> . . . Security of employment;
> Security in retirement;
> Security against misfortune;
> Healthy working conditions;
> Opportunity for advancement;
> Recognition and self-respect.[58]

Security of employment, retirement, and others were factors which demanded

that management take a longer view of the business organization and its

---

[57]Holden, op. cit., pp. 4-5.

[58]Stuart Chase and Others, The Social Responsibility of Management
(New York: School of Commerce, Accounts, and Finance, New York University,
1950), p. 73.

competitive position within the society; management of an organization under a philosophy which neglected the long-run considerations became untenable in terms of the demands that society was placing for economic security.

Concurrently with the evolution of long-range planning concepts there arose an acceptance of the role of the governmental, economic, and social planner in the contemporary world. The radical proponents of the thirties, who proposed the creation of a planned economy operated under a strong centralized administration, had imbued the public with the idea that planning was something done by eccentric academicians bent on the salvation of mankind by a sort of special power of clairvoyance. Such an approach tended to separate the planning individuals from ordinary mortals and as a consequence they were misunderstood and suspected. In the late forties the ill repute in which planning had been recently held disappeared, and heads of corporations, labor leaders, and governmental agencies all began to acknowledge the need for a concept of planning.[59] It is believed that such an acceptance of the necessity and ubiquity of planning concepts was required before business and industry had a climate suitable for the refinement of long-range planning concepts that had been contributed by earlier scholars and thinkers.

During World War II, as corporate managers began to anticipate the post-war markets, planning for conversion to civilian production became a sort of fad. Most of the literature appearing during the war was concerned with various methodology and organizational posture to be utilized in effecting the postwar planning. Many different plans and ideas on

[59] Albert Lepawsky, Administration; The Art and Science of Organization and Management (New York: A. A. Knopf, 1949), pp. 493-494.

planning were presented and one is discouraged with the almost bewilder-
ing mass of proposals and thoughts, which need careful sifting and scrutiny in order to yield a clear concept of what industrial planning was,
how it could be done, and what it could achieve. While World War II created the era of scientific management, World War II was followed by a
vision of planning which became concerned with longer considerations in
terms of the corporate activities. Hempel, in describing the subdivisions
of industrial planning, identified (1) economic; (2) top-management or company orientation planning; and (3) work detail or production planning.
Each, said Hempel, "requires its own technique, methods, and scientific
knowledge."[60] Top management or company orientation planning was considered as the most important sphere of planning insofar as it involved orientation of a company for the long trend, and, "because only on the basis
of this planning can be made those decisions which are expected to insure
the survival and progress of any enterprise within its general and competitive environment."[61] Hempel recognized that top management planning
in the past had been attempted through budgets, sales goals, or quotas,
all of which had been found not quite satisfactory, because, without coordination of the activities of all the company, no assurance was created
for actually achieving the goals.[62] Hempel goes further in describing
the long-range considerations of a firm, and conceives of the problem of
far-future size of the organization as something that need not be defini-

---

[60]Edward H. Hempel, Top-Management Planning; Methods Needed For
Post-War Orientation of Industrial Companies (New York: Harper & Brothers,
1945), p. 4.

[61]Ibid.

[62]Ibid., p. 9.

tized at the beginning of the enterprise but rather should evolve from the
long-range planning processes. While he noted that no definite theory existed on how to determine the potential ultimate size of enterprises, such
things as long-term forecasts, covering periods of more than one year,
would be required. Any well-planned enterprise, he noted, should have a
long-trend concept of size that is being kept in mind and aimed at as an
ultimate long-range goal.[63]

Contributions of Industrial Leaders

Industry leaders, motivated by the requirement for post-war planning, made significant contributions to the evolving concepts of long-
range planning. The lack of plans for expansion of industrial production
required to support the war effort, the optimism manifested in the expected post-war prosperity which seemed to assure a future for the individual
companies worth planning for, and the close relationship between military
and industrial planning during the war caused industrial management groups
to devote more attention to planning for the "far future" of their organizations. In the period of 1941-1945 many companies appointed an organizational entity, or an individual on part-time duty, to study the future of
the company. Specific attention was given to the problem of peacetime
conversion of the existing facilities and the company's organizational
structures. The realization existed that the company involved would, in
all probability, pursue a different type of activity than it had been
drawn into in order to produce defense products. The uneasy peace, and
the subsequent international disruptions of the late forties and early fifties, was nothing more than a suspicion in the minds of a few individuals.

[63]Ibid., p. 25.

The emergence of a new, and seemingly permanent function of long-range planning, was not without difficulties; a dearth of information upon which to base the plans was evident, and few trained executive personnel were available to pursue this differentiated function. Although the fundamental concepts existed, few management groups had a full appreciation of how to employ the new technique. Occasionally an individual, writing in the literature of the time, would present an elementary but yet somewhat integrated approach to the problem. Many executives appeared to have an uneasy realization that present decisions were irrevocably tied in with the extended future of the business; increasing time periods required for product development, and the new marketing techniques, coupled with rising research and development costs, may have forced many executives to give closer attention to the long-run ramifications of their business than they had given in the uneasy thirties.

Charles E. Wilson, president of General Electric in 1940, appointed a "Special Planning Committee" in early 1940 to assume responsibility for planning what the General Electric Company was to do after the war. The committee included representatives from research, engineering, manufacturing, commercial, and accounting departments. As a starting point in its deliberations the committee accepted the postulates of the Atlantic Charter, which stated that opportunity was to be afforded to the people of all countries in developing their own economies. In its initial activities, the committee considered some broad questions relating to the national economics, viz.,

1. State of the country's total output of goods and services, (GNP);

2. Effect of the decline of _laissez faire_ on the American economy;

3. American foreign policy as regards the economic development in European, South American, and other areas of high economic potential;

4. National budgets of production in which the balance between investment and living standards is based on what past experience has shown to be prudent;

5. Relationships among the components of Gross National Output which affected the various parts of the electrical industry and the output of electrical manufacturers.[64]

The committee consisted of three full time (or nearly so) members, with nine advisory members on the special types of company activities having an interest in long-range considerations.[65]

Other industrialists began to recognize the import of long-range planning as ". . . the new and permanent function which war has caused to emerge in each business," and an activity which did not spring from the brain of any single individual, but rather a function which would draw upon the talents of all agencies in the organization.[66] In speaking of this innovation Schell offered a six-point program for long-term planning:

1. An analysis of pre-war activities;

2. Comparison of past and present situations;

3. Definition of current problems requiring attention or decision;

4. A statement of the immediate future outlook;

---

[64]R. P. Gustin and S. A. Holme, "Approach To Post War Planning," Harvard Business Review (July, 1942), pp. 459-472.

[65]Ibid.

[66]E. H. Schell, "Long-Term Company Planning; New Importance to Business," Dun's Review (January, 1943), p. 19.

5. The definition of long-term policy best fitted to encompass future uncertainties and to continue continuity of operation;

6. An adoption of a schedule for periodic examination and review of reports on each element.[67]

He further envisioned the adoption of a schedule for the periodic examination and review of the long-range planning activities of the company.

Other corporations reported reorganizations which were motivated by the need for top management to devote more time to a consideration of the future of business. Typical of this sort of activity was that effected by Johns-Manville Company which relieved its chief executive officer of some of the current operating and management problems. Although there was nothing revolutionary about the reorganization plan, it was unusual in that the chief executive was almost wholly divorced from concern with current operating problems, thereby making it possible for his future time and skill to be devoted to future planning and external relations, leaving the president and the remainder of the staff to operate the business from day to day.[68] Other aspects of Johns-Manville's long-range planning techniques represented a quasi-integrated approach to such activity. Planning was effected for some 1200 items worked out quarterly, annually, and on a five-year basis. Planning started at the lowest echelon with the people who were in actual and constant contact with the

---

[67]Ibid., pp. 17-19.

[68]E. Whitmore, "Organization Plan For Expansion: Johns-Manville Reorganizes Executive Duties," American Business (November, 1946), pp. 56-57.

changing market and gradually worked its way to the top. Finally, it was integrated with similar information originating from other sources in the field.[69]

The accelerated rate of change in all the conditions of commercial enterprise rendered any form of long-term business planning more necessary and more difficult in the postwar period. Many manufacturing companies, some for the first time, began to acknowledge that their sound business decisions of the present often hinged on events and conditions of five, ten, or more years in the future. For some this factor alone was sufficient to justify setting up an agency within the organization to do future planning. Major corporations often were in a more favorable position to do this because of their resources of personnel and capital. In some cases these companies were not primarily manufacturing concerns. The Meredith Publishing Company organized a postwar planning committee during the war which attempted to marshall all available economic fact and opinion relative to the publishing industry and related such information to the company's postwar competitive position.[70] In this company, as in many others, the postwar planning committee, created as a necessity for war production, proved invaluable to management and was appointed as a permanent forward planning committee shortly after the conclusion of hostilities. As would be expected the membership in this committee was drawn from top management personnel with duty thereon performed as a part-time function. As its objective the group was charged with the responsibility of bringing

[69]R. M. Bleiberg, "Industry's Planners - Better Than Government," Barrons (November 18, 1946), p. 3.

[70]S. P. Hall, "Eyes On The Next Decade; A Forward Planning Procedure," NACA Bulletin (December 1, 1948), pp. 375-380.

up to date, and keeping up to date, the work of the predecessor committee
with special emphasis on the possibility and effect of a general recession
sometime in the years ahead. The committee was operated under a philosophy of serving as a stimulus, clearing house, and coordinator for the planning efforts of the entire company. In discharging its responsibilities
as a long-range planning agency, the committee considered its functions
as these:

1. Consulting as appropriate with various department heads on assigned problems;

2. Checking findings and conclusions with outside economic consultants;

3. Submitting findings and conclusions for round table discussions
by all department heads;

4. Submitting to top management for approval all long-range proposals passed on by the committee.

As a fundamental policy the committee continued studying the company's
future position under diverse economic conditions such as war, depression,
inflation, growth, and peace. Tentative plans, policies, and alternative
courses of action were developed for each of the above possible contingencies.[71]

Other companies began to experiment and write about some of the
functional areas of long-range planning, rather than on the general subject matter of future planning. Organization planning was conceived by
the Standard Oil Company of California as the activity of providing the
structure through which work was accomplished in the corporate structure.

---

[71]Ibid.

Such planning was an outgrowth of the depression years and was decentralized to each operating manager in the company who was provided with a staff
to perform the function on a continuing basis. By 1944 long-range organization planning was done on a company-wide basis.[72]

Other economic and legislative factors contributed to the growing
need for a type of long-range planning. An important factor reflecting
this was the enactment by Congress of the Employment Act of 1946 which
provided for a continuing policy and responsibility on the part of the
federal government, to use all practicable means to assure employment opportunities to all those citizens able, willing, and seeking work. This
policy of the government, coupled with the growing influence of the unions
and collective bargaining processes, provided a strong stimulus to business and industry to do more distant planning for factors such as wages,
fringe benefits, and working rules. Many of these considerations had been
short range prior to the second World War.

The growing management literature of the twentieth century, which
began to place more and more emphasis on the role of the top management
group for planning the future of the business, doubtlessly exerted a
strong influence on the development of long-range planning techniques and
processes. More and more businessmen, in executive positions, began to
evaluate critically their role in the organization and in so doing delegated many of the immediate operating problems to their staff agencies.
With this delegation the top management group had sufficient time to give
more thought to the long-term trends of their concerns and in so doing

----

[72]L. L. Purkey, "Organization Planning: A Continuing Job; Standard Oil Company of California; Abstract," *Management Review* (April,
1944), pp. 117-118.

recognized the inadequacy of their organization's preparation for the future. Having recognized the significance of this, they began to study the existing literature on long-range planning. Because of inadequate information available on the subject many were forced to seek help from management consultant agencies and other companies; the very scarcity of literature on the subject in itself tended to inhibit the development of further contemporary literature.

Contributions to Long-Range Planning Thought During 1940-1950

The period of the 1940's provided an opportunity for management thought to be tested and evaluated under diverse forms of economic environment, viz., war-time and peace-time conditions. Close cooperation existed between many segments of the society in order to pursue a common goal of providing ideological and industrial support to the conduct of a global war. It was in this period that the military establishment, and its requirements for a share in the nation's goods and' services, began to exert a profound and continuing influence on the national economy. Contributions to management thought during this period indicated a developing interest in the field of general management; inquiries concerning business objectives served to focus attention on the top management function. The general contributions to long-range planning thought were these:

1. Early in the forties the necessities of war impelled the development of long-range planning concepts in broader terms than had previously existed. Long-term objectives, as necessary guide-posts to organizational activity, became established by progressive companies.

2. Post-war planning committees developed early in the 1940's to prepare business for the coming peace; many such committees gravitated

into a permanent agency within individual companies as a "future demands" group.

3. Compatibility of organizational service objective, social responsibilities of business, and long-range planning were further refined in this period. Union influence, governmental legislation, and the growing emphasis on the role of top-level management in the literature and thought of the period stimulated further study of the future of business.

4. Top-management planning became considered as the most important sphere of planning because of the growing importance of the general and competitive environment. While top-management planning in the past had tended to be concerned with budgets and financial matters, other functional areas began to be studied from a long-term standpoint.

5. Managers began to recognize that many present decisions were tied in with the extended future of the business. Long-range planning was conceived of as a pervasive influence in the firm's philosophy of management and required the talents of all agencies in the organization.

6. For the most part long-range planning was still a concept in the minds of individuals within the organization. The evolving philosophy was not sufficiently developed to be conceived by the institutional mind of the enterprise or in terms of experience larger than that which came to any one individual.

7. Individual company management groups began to visualize their business as a segment of a larger economy operated according to some social and economic plan; growing demands by social groups for more permanency in the economy fostered the development of a high degree of business, government, and social planning.

8. The evolving concepts of long-range planning were broadened in scope and depth; refinement and re-evaluation of techniques and procedures were attempted. Some integration of the functional elements of long-range planning was effected and a basis was laid for the full realization by businessmen of long-range planning as a differentiated and organic function of management.

CHAPTER IV

CONTEMPORARY ASPECTS OF LONG-RANGE PLANNING
IN AMERICAN BUSINESS

Introduction

Contemporary thought concerning long-range planning manifests itself
in the literature of the period and in the practices and policies of business organizations. The thinking on long-range planning is reflected in
how companies are organized for long-range planning; how they were motivated into effecting it, and what approach has been taken in establishing
and operating a long-term planning endeavor. The present chapter examines
the results of primary research carried on by the author. Responses to
the questionnaire are analyzed so as to develop the evolving framework of
the philosophy within contemporary times. The questionnaire was developed
to identify certain factors, forces, and effects which have been influential in the contemporary philosophy of long-range planning. Data presented herein as collected from the questionnaire will be organized around
the following framework:

1. Factors motivating and influencing the development of long-
range planning.

2. The determination of how far ahead to plan.

3. Organizational and procedural arrangements for long-range planning.

4. The accomplishment of long-range planning.

The subsequent chapter will integrate the primary data and observations
with current literature so as to develop the contemporary philosophy of
long-range planning.

The subject of long-range planning is so new that existing literature did not satisfy the author's requirements for depth and coverage
sufficient to develop the contemporary philosophy of long-range planning.
Hence the author used primary research in the form of an extensive questionnaire sent to a representative section of large American corporations.
Appendix B contains a copy of the questionnaire posted as to the total
responses received. Table 2 reflects a summary analysis of the responses
received from the survey. In all, 225 questionnaires were sent out to
various segments of business and industry. Six different types of companies were surveyed: industrials, commercial banks, transportation companies, merchandising firms, utilities, and life insurance companies.
Criteria used in the selection of the companies to receive the questionnaire are reflected in Chapter I and in Appendix A where information-
gathering techniques are also portrayed.

The reader is cautioned not to expect statistical exactness in
portraying the information received in the questionnaire; in some cases
failure of response by a company to a specific question or multiple response to a question created a pattern of answers less than (or more
than) the total number of companies doing long-range planning. Certain
questions required more than one answer, e.g., in the identification of
functional areas in which long-range planning is effected. Statistical
exactness is neither possible nor desired; rather what has been sought
is a measurement of the general trend of long-range planning in the
companies concerned.

TABLE 2

ANALYSIS OF RESPONSES TO QUESTIONNAIRE

Type of Company	No. of Questionnaires Distributed (1)	No. of Companies in Universe (2)	No. of Responses to Questionnaire (3)	No. of Companies not Responding to Questionnaire (4)	No. of Companies Not Performing LRP (5)	No. of Companies Performing LRP (6)	No. of Companies Responding but not Contributing (7)	Percentage Res- of Respondents Doing LRP (8)
Industrials	150	500	61	89	3	55	3	90%
Merchandising Firms	15	50	8	7		6	2	75%
Utilities	15	50	7	8		7		100%
Commercial Banks	15	50	6	9	1	5		83%
Life Insurance Co's.	15	50	5	10	3	2		40%
Transportation Co's.	15	50	4	11		4		100%
Totals	225	750	91	134	7	79	5	86.4%

Note: Column (7) reflects total of 5 respondents that declined to participate in the study. It is not known whether these companies perform long-range planning. Column (8) computed by dividing Column (6) by Column (3).

Factors Motivating and Influencing the Development of

Long-Range Planning

Certain factors and forces motivated the emergence of long-term planning in American businesses. Various methods were used to establish the initial long-range planning effort. Some companies have not entered into long-range planning for certain reasons of corporate policy and industry influences. Before discussing these areas the extent of long-range planning in American business should be examined in order that the reader may gain an appreciation for the magnitude of this phenomenon in certain contemporary businesses.

Extent of Long-Range Planning in American Business

Formal long-range planning as a post-war phenomenon is practiced to varying degrees depending upon the type of company involved. All transportation and utility companies responding to the survey indicate that long-range planning is conducted. As may be noted from Table 2, industrials, merchandising firms, and commercial banks report that a majority of such companies effect long-range planning. Life insurance companies report a low incident of long-range planning. In effecting long-range planning a business corporation has several alternatives relative to the development of specific plans or of just one best long-range plan for the corporation. Table 3 indicates the practice of contemporary business in the creation of an alternative versus one best long-range plan. As may be noted from this table the majority of the businesses create alternative long-range plans as opposed to the formulation of just one best long-range plan. However, a significant number do endeavor to establish just one best long-range plan. In all probability companies doing long-range planning establish alternative plans and evaluate them in the selection of the one best plan. Nothing is reflected in the questionnaire to substantiate this, however; rather, this is an assumption of the author.

TABLE 3

COMPANIES REPORTING CREATION OF <u>ALTERNATIVE</u> VS <u>ONE BEST</u>
LONG-RANGE PLAN

	Alternative Plans	One Best LRP
Industrial	37	18
Utilities	5	2
Merchandising Firms	3	3
Commercial Banks	3	2
Transportation Co's.	3	1
Life Insurance Co's.	2	0
Totals	53	26

TABLE 4

ANALYSIS OF COMPANIES REPORTING GROWTH AND CONTRACTION PLANS

	Contraction and Growth Plans	Growth Plans Only
Industrials	47	8
Utilities	4	3
Merchandising Firms	2	4
Commercial Banks	4	1
Transportation Co's.	4	0
Life Insurance Co's.	2	0
Totals	63	16

A significant majority of the companies engaged in long-range planning report the development of contraction as well as growth plans. Table 4 shows the analysis of companies reporting the development of growth and contraction plans. Merchandising firms report the greatest propensity to develop only growth plans as opposed to contraction and growth plans. Several observations and conclusions can be drawn from this Table. In spite of the optimism of corporate leaders as to the growth opportunities in the expanding American economy a significant number of business firms do long-term planning which appears to take into consideration the contingency of a downturn in business activity. Contemporary companies are effecting their long-range planning so as to have flexibility in order that an orderly withdrawal of the factors of production can be efficiently accomplished. The long-range planning that is effected appears to have a high degree of flexibility and is adaptable to changing economic conditions.

There appears to be a trend to the creation of a master long-range plan for individual company use based upon the number of companies reporting the development of such a plan for all major functional areas of the business. As may be noted from Table 5 over half of the industrials report the creation of a master plan. Most of the other types of companies indicate that a master plan is created; commercial banks report no existence of a master plan.

Long-range planning is a continuous effort in the majority of the companies responding. Table 6 reflects whether the respondents effect long-range planning on a continuous or intermittent basis. As a continuous effort the activity is presumably performed by a full time staff agency specifically appointed for the long-range planning corporate effort. Long-range planning, in its infancy, was probably performed as an additional duty by a top management official. It was also probably effected on an intermittent basis as the executive had other problems such as the immediate task of planning, organizing, and controlling the day-to-day operational activities. As more time was given to future

factors, however, long-range planning staffs were appointed and long-range

planning as a formal activity became conducted on a continuous basis.

TABLE 5

FREQUENCY OF COMPANIES REPORTING DEVELOPMENT OF A MASTER LONG-RANGE
PLAN FOR ALL MAJOR FUNCTIONAL AREAS

	Master Plan Created	No Master Plan
Industrials	35	15
Utilities	5	2
Merchandise Firms	4	2
Transportation Companies	1	2
Commercial Banks	0	3
Life Insurance Companies	1	1
Totals	46	25

Note: Eight companies reported as engaged in long-range planning did
not answer this question; consequently it is presumed that their long-
range planning may not be sufficiently refined to formulate a master plan.

TABLE 6

COMPANIES REPORTING ON CONTINUOUS OR INTERMITTENT
FREQUENCY OF LONG-RANGE PLANNING

	Continuous	Intermittent
Industrial	42	15
Utilities	5	3
Merchandise Firms	2	4
Commercial Banks	2	3
Transportation Companies	3	1
Life Insurance Companies	2	0
Totals	56	26

Note: Three companies reported both continuous and intermittent long-
range planning.

Internal Company Conditions

In the questionnaire companies were requested to give a narrative answer as to why they had initiated a long-range planning effort. The answers received were varied and complex; quantification was not possible or desirable as the author sought only the general qualitative factors as to why the long-range planning effort was established. These answers have been categorized as to internal and external factors and further classified when possible into a qualitative structure based upon the general type of reason for initiating long-range planning.

Internal company conditions necessitating the development of a long-range planning activity are varied and complex. Company growth and complexity, diverse production activities, and a complex technology characterized by long product lead times are significant internal factors stimulating the establishment of a formal planning organization in the corporations. Long-range planning effort has been undertaken to motivate existing management to do more long-range thinking and planning, to determine future manufacturing requirements, and to permit evaluation of new product development. Several general intracorporate factors give impetus to the evolving philosophy of long-range planning:

1. Trend to industrial decentralization. The trend to more decentralization in industry fostered the development of a formal structure for long-range planning. A formal structure was required to coordinate and relate the decentralization of corporate product efforts among many relatively autonomous and functionally integrated divisions. Underlying this change was the increased scope and magnitude of company operations and the greater complexity and diversity of the product mix.

The existence of a company decentralization policy, coupled with growth
and diversification, stimulated the need for the establishment and cen-
tralization of long-range planning functions. Approaching stagnation in
profit divisions and the change from a homogeneous one-industry company
to a diversified, decentralized structure further motivated the desire
to develop a far-future planning effort.

2. Company growth and complexity. In the case of a highly di-
visionalized company there is a tendency for each division to optimize
its own operations and plans as it understands them without full knowledge of the corporate activity directed toward the same goal. When the
company is small this total corporate coordination is relatively simple
and effective; as the firm grows it is more and more time-consuming for
top management to perform this function unaided; a gradual evaluation to
more formalized handling of this responsibility is to be expected. Thus
the long-range planning effort, effected by a staff agency, evolves.

3. Internal dissatisfaction with decentralized unit and corporate profit margins. Over-concentration of sales in one general product
line or a need for growth and diversification at an accelerated rate to
overcome the depressing effect of the declining sales of one product
motivated the need for long-range planning.

4. Growing obsolescence of equipment, aging of key executive
personnel and ultimate retirement of founders are other reasons for long-
range planning. It appears that the long-range planning effort followed
a decision that the company should step up expansion to capitalize on
opportunities available to it. Doubtlessly the introduction of younger
management groups imbued with professional management education fostered
the long-range planning development.

Many diverse reasons were given as internal factors or forces stimulating a long-range planning need. A few additional reasons are cited to reflect the heterogeneity of causal factors:

Prior commitment to a growth program together with a systematic capital conservation program which had produced sizable reserves.

Prudent allocation of resources for rationally selected company sponsored research and development programs.

Changing concepts in our industry brought about changing internal requirements.

Belief that planning was an essential management tool.

It was recognized that a planning staff was required for product improvement, for development of new designs and for the initiation of new studies.

It is difficult to separate the internal and external factors which caused business organizations to develop a long-range planning capability. In most cases the internal and external environment is so intertwined that a type of interdependency exists. As noted by one respondent to the study:

In the face of rapid technological change, with its associated shift in market emphasis from manned aircraft to guided missiles, the internal organization of the company appeared inadequately structured to forge an effective coordination and communication network between research, development and engineering on the one hand, and marketing and customer relations on the other. Consequently, there seemed to be a need for a formal long-range planning activity, two of whose objectives were to effect a better coordination between these functions and to provide a longer time perspective applicable to both.

In the utility industry long-range planning has existed longer than in the other types of industries studied in this paper.[1] Some of the basic characteristics of that industry dictated an early development of long-range planning, viz., (a) plant investment in a utility is substantially larger than for other industries; (b) long equipment life,

e.g., the expected life of an electric utility plant will range from
30 to 45 years; (c) lack of mobility on the part of a utility since the
territory served is fixed by franchise agreement, and also the market
for a utility's product tends to be stable; furthermore, major investments are in plant installations which, in general, cannot readily or
economically be moved; (d) maximum earnings are regulated by state com-
missions and many other functions and characteristics of utility service are regulated by state and federal governmental bodies.

In conclusion the internal factors which caused business organizations to develop a long-range planning capability are varied and complex.
In general the need arose because of the influence played by the external
environment; in most respects the planning capability that was developed
followed the response of intra-company activities to extra-organizational
considerations.

External Factors which Created Need for Long-Range Planning

Several factors and forces exist which created the need for the
organized, systematic and functional activity that is called long-range
planning. External factors of a national, industrial, and competitive
nature which motivated the development of a long-range planning activity
in the participating organizations are varied. Narrative answers to the
questionnaire in this respect were varied and defy precise quantification
and classification; consequently the author has chosen to classify these

------

[1]See Table 7, p. 125.

reasons into the following component parts and to discuss them in the
order reflected herein:

1. Competitive elements.
2. Availability of planning data and tools.
3. Union influences.
4. Social factors.
5. Production techniques.
6. Governmental considerations.

Competitive elements. Competitive elements motivating the need
for long-range planning include such factors as the expansion of markets
and increasing competition particularly since World War II. Increasing
research and development costs incurred in order to keep pace with the
dynamic move of technological change, coupled with the rise of research
and innovation in all fields of functional work required a revision of
existing planning policies and procedures of the competitive business
enterprise. In order to remain competitive the firm was required to increase its research commitments in "frontier products"; financial outlays
involved for the research and development programs became so huge that
long-range planning became necessary so the expenditures involved were
compatible to the probabilities of the payoff. The decline in funding
for traditional products, coupled with an increasing product obsolescence and an increased demand fostered by an expansion of markets, made
a longer view mandatory for business units. As technology increased
and products became more complex, the period required for product development leadtime increased; product substitutes were offered with increasing frequency both from domestic and foreign sources. Higher capital
costs were incurred and profit margins were reduced accordingly. Collateral with these changes the business unit increased in size and complexity; the number and rapidity of major changes affecting business

increased. Business became more competitive through (1) diversification by other firms; (2) saturation of markets and excess capacity; (3) competitors' innovations, improvements, and new strategies; (4) foreign production; (5) increasing size and term of capital commitments.

Another factor explaining the attention to long-range planning is that financial analysts in search of growth companies have reacted favorably to situations where management has attempted to forecast the specific shape and scope of potential growth and then has taken positive action in anticipation of future demands. Maines, in a study conducted for the Stanford Research Institute, found a definite relationship between a company's growth and its forward looking programs to promote its future in such areas as product development, market development, company acquisitions, and other long-range factors.[2] The fact that some of the leading corporations in the country developed a philosophy of long-range planning no doubt forced competitors to do likewise in order to compete adequately.

Availability of planning data and tools. While competitive elements have played a significant factor in motivating American business to initiate a long-range planning effort it is worth noting that one of the reasons long-range planning activity has expanded is because there is available today a large body of data and descriptive information which did not exist some years ago. There has been an expansion in coverage and improvement in the quality of government statistics, trade information, professional publications, and independent research related to

---

[2]N. R. Maines, Why Companies Grow (Menlo Park, Calif.: Stanford Research Institute, 1957), p. 2.

business. Government statistics have improved in coverage and quality in the last decade; the continued growth and involvement of the government in economic matters promises to provide more statistical data for business use in the future.

Recent innovations in computer techniques, and the formulation of mathematical models, ecological models, business games, and related planning and control tools have also doubtlessly had a favorable effect on the evolving philosophy of long-range planning.

Union influences. Trade unions since World War II have influenced corporate management in many areas. Company executive personnel are restricted in their activities with the work force; legislation and social pressures have all but eliminated arbitrary and capricious action with respect to the worker. The demands of unions for security, stability, and fringe benefits have forced management to do more planning than was done prior to World War II. Labor costs have tended to become fixed, thus creating some additional impediments to flexibility which earlier management groups had. Contracts entered into through the collective bargaining process have become "long-term" in the sense of extending several years into the future. The restrictions of the labor contracts, growing fringe benefits, provisions for guaranteed annual wages, contributions for supplemental unemployment benefits, and many other lesser union demands have dictated that long-range planning for labor costs be conducted. Cooperating companies in this study indicated that long-range planning for labor and associated costs is conducted five or more years into the future.[3]

---

[3]See pages 136-141.

Social factors. As a group in American society, social factors
have affected management's role in coordinating the factors of production in the business environment. The demands of society for stability
of employment and security within the economy have caused business leaders to become more concerned about their organization's destiny; management has taken on increased responsibility with respect to the stability
and welfare of the community in which the company operates. Other factors, more subtle perhaps, have given the business leader no practical
alternative except to take a long-range point of view. Pressures of
changing population have stimulated business leaders to search for a solution to increased productivity through forward-looking investments in
automation and other technological improvements. The determination of
the American people that steadily rising levels of living and economic
stability are both desirable and achievable has encouraged a greater
social responsibility in businessmen.

Other social and political factors played a significant part in
the creation of a "need" for long-range planning. Perhaps one of the
most important influences was the changing managerial philosophy that
emerged in response to the demands of the 1950-1961 business environment.
The time span of managerial decisions has been lengthening so fast as to
make necessary a systematic exploration of the uncertainty and risk of
future decisions. Drucker, in speaking of the essentiality of time di-
mensioned decisions, notes:

> Today practically every manager takes ten or twenty year risks
> without wincing. He takes them in product development, in re-
> search, in market development, in the development of a sales or-
> ganization, and in almost anything. This lengthening of the
> time span of commitment is one of the most significant features
> of our age. It underlies our economic advances. But while

quantitative in itself, it has changed the qualitative character of entrepreneural decisions. It has, so to speak, converted time from being a dimension in which business decisions are being made into an essential element of the decisions themselves.[4]

Another external force operating in the managerial environment was the optimistic belief by industry leaders in their company's growth and the ability of the economy to grow. Underlying this concept was the development by professional management of the idea of looking ahead. Business respondents indicate an attitude of being "expansion minded" and thus implement long-range planning in order to meet the growth objectives. Growth in a specific industry was often attained through a merger or consolidation to effect diversification. As the business became larger and more complex a form of divisionalization and decentralization became imperative. With decentralization the planning problem became complex and it was necessary to appoint a long-range planning staff to coordinate the total corporate goals.

Production techniques. Production techniques and the recent changes thereto influenced long-range planning. Increasing mechanization and automation, stimulated by technological influences in manufacturing methods and processes, required long-range planning by management groups before committing the large capital outlay required to support these programs. In the post-war era, United States industry has engaged in a massive drive to replace men by machines. This has cut the cost of production labor; but fixed costs have gone up sharply. The replacement of labor with capital equipment has, because of the

---

[4]Peter F. Drucker, "Long-Range Planning: Challenge To Management Science," Management Science (April, 1959), p. 241.

long-term commitment of resources, forced management to do more planning.
The corporation with heavy fixed charges is less flexible in a downturn
than was the same company with workers instead of machines. The logic
is simply that workers could be laid off but it is more difficult to remove the fixed charges.

Governmental considerations. Governmental considerations and increasing expenditures for national defense have fostered intimate contact
between military and industrial leaders; consequently the military concept of planning has been influential. In addition the budgeting procedures of the Department of Defense, the advent of space technology and
warfare, and the decline in funding for traditional military products
have affected a large segment of American industry, particularly those
engaged in defense work. As the president of a large west coast defense
contractor noted in a letter to the author as to why his company had developed a formal long-range planning effort:

> The increasing complexity and consequent rising cost of defense
> products, the extension of the technological base underlying
> product development, the trend toward longer and more costly
> development cycles, and the more rapid technical obsolescence
> of products and capabilities. In addition, changes in policy
> on the part of the defense establishment were beginning to
> emerge, exemplified by placing on defense contractors a greater
> responsibility for financing their own working capital and
> their long-range capital investments in research facilities
> and company-initiated research and development activities.
> These external factors pointed up the need for a more system-
> atic study of long-term trends in the defense business and for
> sharper tools for selecting from among long-term investment
> opportunities.

Another company, in indicating why it developed an advanced planning

staff, said:

> During the Korean War, this company was a major supplier of
> helicopters to the military. In the post-Korea period, mili-
> tary sales were practically insignificant and steps had to be
> taken to develop commercially suitable aircraft while at the
> same time developing aircraft for possible future military
> use. Our advanced planning staff formed the nucleus for
> these endeavors.

Reasons for not Conducting Long-Range Planning

As might be expected, not all companies agree that long-range

planning is feasible and practical. Volatile labor conditions, frequent

price changes, cyclical demand, unstable consumer preference, and gov-

ernment controls are cited as reasons for not effecting any degree of

long-range planning. Many companies consider various long-run factors

in their operational (short-range) planning but such is done on an in-

formal basis without a definite program such as is considered in a for-

mal long-range planning endeavor. In certain segments of business speci-

fic formal long-range planning programs have not been adopted to any de-

gree. For example, in the life insurance business there appears to be

some informal long-range planning with a tendency to the development of

more formal techniques, as evidenced by the fact that only 40 per cent

of the life insurance companies responding to the survey indicate exist-

ence of long-range planning. The recent attention to future planning

has doubtlessly stimulated interest in long-range aspects of the life

insurance business with a consequent establishment of planning objec-

tives but no formal programs of accomplishment.

Some quasi long-range planning is accomplished which consists pri-

marily of an analysis of market and technological data for specific purposes and with respect to one product or a group of products as distinct from a continuous systematic effort. This type of _ad hoc_ long-range planning appears as a predecessor to formalized, continuous long-range planning effort within the corporate structure. Such _ad hoc_ planning for the far future has its pitfalls; one of the greatest is inability to relate the effort to all segments of the company on a continuous basis and with respect to an overall long-term objective.

One company reported unique product and demand differences which influence its approach to long-term planning. This company, in the packaging industry, indicated:

> This is a highly volatile business and it is difficult, if not impracticable, to plan too far in advance. Much of the demand for our products is closely tied to food product manufacture and sales. As a result, our business is more dependent upon short term population trends than upon national and international economic or political trends.
>
> Secondly, product development time in the packaging industry is extremely short compared to other industries. A new package can often be designed, constructed and sold in less than a year. With such a short lead time, long-range planning as such is hardly applicable.
>
> Thirdly, in most cases, ideas for new package designs stem directly from our customers' needs rather than from internally developed ideas although we do have extensive product and basic research facilities.[5]

There appears to be a tacit assumption that the changing market conditions as affected by economic influences outside the control of management are so significant that any long-range planning effort is fruitless and at best simply a defensive measure. In all probability some managers are too preoccupied with current problems to devote creative thought to developing the company's future. The uncertainty of

-----

[5]Letter, Continental Can Company, Inc., dated Feb. 27, 1962.

future business trends and the influence played by unpredictable events
such as the Berlin crisis discourages some companies from doing any
long-range planning. One company official indicated that it is more
important for the organization to remain flexible instead of "straight-
jacketing itself" into a fixed plan.

Examples of astigmatic and unproductive long-range planning which
did not result in any future advantage for the company exist. Two classic
examples may be cited:

1. Five years ago, several international airlines placed orders
for jet transports based on an anticipated number of future air passengers
determined through long-range planning decisions. Today, with the jet
transports delivered, many of the new aircraft are flying with passenger
loads well under capacity.

2. The ill-starred Edsel is another example. An enormous amount
of planning preceded its debut. Among other things, the Ford Motor Co.
employed teams of sociologists from three universities to survey consumer motives for buying cars. Since planning for the introduction of a
single product can go so far off the track, the anti-planners say it's
even more futile to try to map all of a company's future moves in a
single document.[6]

While these companies sustained losses because of a failure of
their long-range plans to materialize as envisioned, the losses may have
been relatively greater if no long-range planning had been effected.
As is evidenced from Table 2 of a total of 91 companies responding to

[6]The Wall Street Journal, October 25, 1961.

the questionnaire seven companies indicated that no long-range planning as envisioned in this paper was effected. Life insurance companies reported most frequently the absence of long-range planning activities.

In summary the absence of long-range planning as reported in this study by the seven companies claiming no long-range planning may be attributed to:

1. Volatile environmental changes in labor, demand, price, and governmental activities.

2. Cyclical business conditions adversely affecting concerned companies.

3. Unique product and demand conditions.

4. Extremely short product development time as compared to other industries.[7]

5. Preoccupation on the part of management with operational or short-run problems.

6. The uncertainty of future business trends; the influence of significant and unpredictable national and international events.

Establishment of the Long-Range Planning Effort

The establishment of the long-range planning effort in the individual companies varied as to the type of company involved. Corporations cooperating in the study were requested to indicate the year in which they initiated "somewhat formal" long-range planning within their company or its ancestral company. The responses to this query are indi-

---

[7]This factor was reported twice as a reason why a polled company did not effect long-range planning.

cated in Table 7. While some companies report that they initiated long-range planning several decades ago the majority of the long-range planning effort began in the period 1950-1961.[8]

TABLE 7

YEAR IN WHICH PARTICIPATING COMPANIES BEGAN EFFECTING
LONG-RANGE PLANNING

Type of Company	Prior to 1920	1920 to 1930	1930 to 1940	1940 to 1950	1950 to 1960	1960 thru 1961
Industrials		1	1	8	37	7
Commercial Banks					3	2
Transportation Cos.			1	1	1	1
Merchandising Firms					5	1
Utilities		2	1	3	1	
Life Insurance Cos.	1					1
Totals	1	3	3	12	47	12

Utilities indicated that long-range planning was initiated in that industry somewhat earlier than in the other industries. Of the two life insurance companies that reported a long-range planning effort one company indicated that its long-range planning effort was established in 1868, the year of the company founding. This probably means that a type of mental long-range planning of some degree was carried on by the company officials, but it is doubted if such effort was the formalized activity envisioned in this paper. Although the long-range planning effort was undertaken in a majority of the companies during the period 1950 through 1960, a significant number indicated that long-range planning was initiated in the preceding decade; twelve companies representing all

---

[8]The author qualified this interrogation with the modifying phrase "somewhat formal long-range planning" to identify that type of long-range planning that was done formally by an organizational entity and/or an individual specifically assigned for long-range planning. It was believed that to simply have asked "When did you initiate long-range planning?" would have elicited a response which considered the long-range informal planning that has probably always characterized top management planning. Such a response would have been misleading to the study.

types of companies except utilities initiated long-range planning in the period 1960-1961. The findings in this study support the claim in existing management literature that long-range planning is a post World War II phenomenon. The establishment of formal long-range planning effort in American business implies that a specific organizational structure may have been selected to perform this function from its inception; in the study cooperating companies were asked as to when they established a specific organizational entity for the long-range planning effort. The responses to this interrogation are indicated in Table 8.

TABLE 8

YEAR IN WHICH PARTICIPATING COMPANIES ESTABLISHED SPECIFIC
ORGANIZATIONAL ENTITY FOR LONG-RANGE PLANNING

Type of Company	Prior to 1920	1920 to 1930	1930 to 1940	1940 to 1950	1950 to 1960	1960 thru 1961
Industrials				2	28	13
Commercial Banks						
Transportation Cos.				1	1	1
Merchandising Firms					3	3
Utilities	3			3	1	
Life Insurance Cos.					1	1
Totals	3			6	34	18

This table seems to indicate that business, in implementing a somewhat formal long-range planning effort, appointed a specific organizational structure, responsibility, and authority to carry out this differentiated function of management. The establishment of a specific organizational entity for long-range planning somewhat closely parallels the same time period in which long-range planning was established by the companies.

The establishment of the initial long-range planning effort was approached in a variety of ways. Management consultant agencies, trade associations, American Management Association seminars, and similar sources of assistance were sought; Table 9 shows the various ways in which the companies obtained assistance. As may be noted major dependence was placed on the creative ability of company personnel. The study of other companies' methods and the gleaning of material from current periodical and book literature also played a significant part in establishing the initial effort. Only six instances of government assistance were reported; universities and colleges and management consultant agencies also provided assistance to companies involved in establishing a long-range planning effort.

TABLE 9

METHOD USED TO ESTABLISH INITIAL LONG-RANGE PLANNING EFFORT

Method	Frequency Method Reported
Depended upon Creative Ability of Company Personnel	73
Studied Other Companies' Methods	49
Studied Current Periodical and Book Literature	49
Sought Help from Management Consultant Agencies	22
Sought Help from Universities and Colleges	14
Sought Help from Government Agencies	6

Concurrent with the task of setting up the long-range planning effort business was concerned with changing the attitudes of middle and lower management to appreciate and support the evolving philosophy of long-range planning. In this respect one company interviewed reported no problem of selling the organization on the concept of having their planning done for them by a separate staff because the entire organization was alert to the necessity for new products and new processes so that management at all levels continuously considered new directions for development. Several alternatives and methods are available to enjoin the wholehearted cooperation of management groups. Suitable policy instruments may be published, formal instruction on the subject may be given, executive persuasion exercised, or formal seminars conducted. The frequency of practice in using the above alternatives as reported by the respondents is reflected in Table 10.

TABLE 10

METHOD USED BY COMPANIES TO GAIN MIDDLE AND LOWER MANAGEMENT
SUPPORT FOR LONG-RANGE PLANNING

Method	Frequency
Executive Persuasion	48
Published Suitable Policy Instruments	33
Conducted Seminars in LRP within the Company	25
Formal Instruction in LRP Activities for Executive Personnel	9

Although planning is considered an integral part of the management function the degree to which the activity is standardized or formalized may be left to the discretion of individual managers. Support of middle and lower managers is either inherent or may be won by the persuasion of a planning-minded chief; a more formal method of enlisting certain executive support is required as evidenced by the number of companies which indicate that suitable policy instruments are published to cover long-range planning. Formal instruction in long-range planning activities for executive personnel is a method least used by business; in all probability the reason for the infrequent use of this method is because long-range planning is so new a concept that few qualified people exist to provide the necessary formal instruction. One company interviewed claimed that the initial interest in long-range planning as a formalized function originated at the middle levels of management and the real problem was

to enlist top management support. Another company reported that the corporate top management group required that decisions concerning markets,
products, organization, and the acquisition and allocation of resources
(e.g., research and facilities budgets) having a long-term impact upon
future company activities be supported and justified by long-range planning analyses. One company reported that the long-range planning function was an outgrowth and amplification of the existing system of annual
budgeting and, as such, support was gained through having managers develop
and support their annual and long-term budgets. Another company reported
that the company requirement existed that all echelons establish long and
short term objectives and then periodically report on the progress toward
such goals; such a requirement developed in subordinate echelon management personnel an appreciation of the importance and logic of long-range
planning.

There is some indication that emphasizing participation in long-
range planning activities is an important way of gaining support for
long-range planning; such participation ranged from classroom attendance
to actual engagement in the long-range planning activities, either in a
seminar or through executive contact.

The Time Elements of Long-Range Planning

Long and short-range planning are somewhat similar in technique and application; the basic difference is in the time dimensions thereof. Contemporary literature frequently refers to long-range planning as that planning which is extended one or more years into the future. The question arises as to what the experience of business has been in this respect; the following section will examine this area.

Determining How Far Ahead to Plan

Complex factors determine both the functional and the overall corporate planning period; some of the important determinants are the industry peculiarities, the market demand, the availability of resources, the lead time involved in the product life cycle and the specific objectives of the corporation. In speaking of "how far ahead corporations plan" caution must be exercised to clarify whether one is speaking of the overall corporate long-range planning period, of the planning period for a specific functional area of effort, or of another element of long-range planning, e.g., the availability of raw materials.

The length of the future period for which long-term plans should be made is a technical factor of the first magnitude. As a rule the planning period should be based on an economic projection which follows normal trends without regard to cyclical fluctuations of the economy. A company should plan as far ahead as is useful but only so far as it is possible to do so with reasonable accuracy. As regards overall corporate long-range planning the respondent companies indicated the periods reflected in Table 11.

Most literature cites three to five years as the most common overall long-range planning term. However, if one is speaking of the overall corporate long-range planning period how is such "overall planning period" determined? Several alternative methods of determining this period are available, e.g.,

1. The average planning period for the conglomerate functional area of effort;

2. The longest single period of functional area long-range planning;

3. The time period required to provide for raw materials;

4. An arbitrary period which in the judgment of the executive group best fits the long-range objectives of the firm;

5. A period which encompasses the most critical areas of long-range planning within the corporation;

6. A period which provides for the best market advantage in terms of economic cycles and long-term growth.

TABLE 11

OVERALL CORPORATE LONG-RANGE PLANNING PERIOD

Period Involved	Frequency Period Reported
Over 5 years	45
Over 10 years	21
Over 3 years	14
Over 1 year	7
Over 20 years	3
Over 50 years	2
Over 30 years	0

The determinants of the long-range planning period for a particular company can be determined by evaluation of the factors which dictate the

term from which plans are formulated. Table 12 reflects the factors determining length of period corporations plan ahead.

TABLE 12

FACTORS DETERMINING LENGTH OF PERIOD CORPORATIONS PLAN AHEAD

Determinant	Frequency Reported
Market Development Time	58
Product Development Time	43
Facilities Construction Time	37
Availability of Accurate Data	31
Pay-Off Time for Capital Investment	27
Capital Acquisition Time	21
Raw Materials Availability	12

According to respondents market development time plays the most
significant role as a factor determining the length of the planning period. Product development time and facilities construction time are also
important factors dictating the term of planning. Raw materials availability plays a relatively minor role in this respect, although it should
be recognized that with some companies this may be a major determinant.
It may be considered minor by other companies because of the general
availability of the raw materials they use. Availability of accurate
data and the pay-off time for capital investment are significant factors
influencing the planning period.

Most companies report that the present period for which long-range
plans are developed is suitable as evidenced by answers to the question:
Do you contemplate extending or contracting the period for which long-
range plans are developed, Answers to this question were:

Present period suitable   59
Will extend   15
Will contract   0

No company reported an intention to contract the period; reasons given
for extending the period were the long-development cycles required for
new products and the increasingly heavy company commitments in capital
investments and in research undertakings. Presumably, however, improvements in market intelligence, in forecasting techniques, and in other
long-range planning processes would be required before the period could
be extended.

Planning Area Period Determinants

The planning periods for the functional and other areas of long-
range planning reflect that significantly different time periods are
used for planning in the same functional areas within the same industry.
Tables 13 through 18 reflect the period of planning by cooperating organizations broken down by the type of company involved. Raw materials
sources and real estate tend to be planned for a greater period into
the future. In general long-range planning in functional and other
areas is planned most frequently for periods of five and ten years although a considerable number of companies report planning in the areas
for periods of two and three years. Relatively few companies indicate
planning for periods of four, six, seven, eight, or nine years. A lumber processing company reported that three farms are planned on a basis
of tree maturity in excess of fifty years.

In analyzing the tables several general findings may be derived.
First the major functional and additional areas of effort reflect a similarity of planning period. Practically all of the areas reflect planning that is projected beyond a one year period thus indicating that a
long-range planning philosophy has become a pervasive influence in busi-

ness and industry and that it takes into consideration a wide range of
corporate effort involved in a business organization. Also the findings
substantiate the assumption stated earlier that the period for long-
range planning is clearly a function of the area of effort under consideration. Consequently, in speaking of the corporate planning period one
should relate this to the area under consideration in the planning activity. The tables also point out that there should be some logic in
selecting the right time range for a company's planning; in all probability a company should not plan for a period longer than is economically justifiable. Koontz and O'Donnell have developed the "commitment
principle" or the concept that planning should encompass the period of
time necessary to fulfill the commitments involved.[9] This implies that
there is no uniform or arbitrary length of time for which a given company should plan but rather that the period is based on various plans
depending on the commitment involved.

As may be observed in Tables 13 through 18 many of the companies
failed to report how far ahead planning is conducted in the appropriate
areas. This seems to indicate that although a large majority of the
companies effect long-range planning, there is some indecision as to how
far ahead planning is actually conducted.

Complex factors determine both the functional and the overall corporate planning period. While there appears to be a somewhat arbitrary
selection of planning periods by businessmen, some uniformity exists between the planning periods of the major functional areas of effort.

---

[9]Harold Koontz and Cyril O'Donnell, Principles of Management (New
York: McGraw-Hill Book Company, Inc., 1959), p. 468.

The author has not made an attempt to differentiate intermediate planning from long-range and short-range planning. Davis, of the Ohio State University, has said that intermediate planning has to do largely with planning the work of <u>organizing</u> for the short-range execution of long-range plans. The latter are modified as progress is made through time toward the point in time of execution. The need for intermediate planning is suggested in the three year minor mode in the frequencies of planning periods reflected in Table 13 through 18.[10]

---

[10]See pp. 36-41.

TABLE 13

PERIOD OF PLANNING BY SELECTED CORPORATIONS
(Industrials)

Area of Planning	Corporate Frequency of Planning by Period (Stated in Years)												
	1	2	3	4	5	6	7	8	9	10	15	20	50
Product Research & Development		1	4	1	27					8	1	1	
Product Costing	2	2	6		21					3			
Facilities	1	3	4		24	2				8	1		
Manufacturing/Production	2	6	4		20	2				6			
Finance		4	3	1	20	2				10			
Credit	2	2	2		10	2							
Marketing	2	3	4	1	25					10			
Organizational Structure	3	5	5		17					4			
Executive Development	2	3	1		18					8	1		
Industrial Relations	4	3	3		10					4			
Personnel	5	6	3		11					5			
Policy Formulation	2	1	3		11					5			
Public Relations	9	2	3		9					4			
Sources of Raw Materials	1	2	3		11					3	3	1	1
Sources of Supplies	1	2	4		9					2			
Subcontracting	3	2	3		6					3			
Product Distribution	3	1	1		17					3			
Charity Contributions	11	2	1		7					2			
Product Engineering		5	5		15					4			
Real Estate		1	3		10					7	1	2	
Mfg. Methods & Processes	1	2	3		18	2				7			
Product Competition	1			4	19					18			
Advertising	9	5	2		9					2			
"Size Planning"					8	2				17			

TABLE 14

PERIOD OF PLANNING BY SELECTED CORPORATIONS
(Transportation Companies)

Area of Planning	Corporate Frequency of Planning by Period (Stated in Years)												
	1	2	3	4	5	6	7	8	9	10	15	20	25
Product Research & Developmt						1				1			
Product Costing	1				1								
Facilities										1			1
Manufacturing/Production	1				1								
Finance					1					1			
Credit													
Marketing	1				1								
Organizational Structure	1												
Executive Development												1	
Industrial Relations			1										
Personnel												1	
Policy Formulation	1												
Public Relations	1												
Sources of Raw Materials													
Sources of Supplies	1												
Subcontracting	1												
Product Distribution	1												
Charity Contributions	1												
Product Engineering		1											
Real Estate											1		
Mfg. Methods & Processes	1												
Product Competition		1											
Advertising		1											
"Size Planning"					1								

TABLE 15

PERIOD OF PLANNING BY SELECTED CORPORATIONS
(Utilities)

Area of Planning	Corporate Frequency of Planning by Period (Stated in Years)												
	1	2	3	4	5	6	7	8	9	10	15	20	25
Product Research & Developt					1								
Product Costing			1		1								
Facilities					3					1		1	
Manufacturing/Production			2		1								
Finance			2		1							2	
Credit	1												
Marketing	2				1							2	
Organizational Structure					1					1			
Executive Development										1			
Industrial Relations					1								
Personnel					1					1			
Policy Formulation					1								
Public Relations					1								
Sources of Raw Materials			2							1		1	
Sources of Supplies					2								
Subcontracting			1										
Product Distribution		1			3								
Charity Contributions													
Product Engineering					1								
Real Estate			2								2	2	
Mfg. Methods & Processes					1								
Product Competition			2		2							2	
Advertising	1												
"Size Planning"													

TABLE 16

PERIOD OF PLANNING BY SELECTED CORPORATIONS
(Life Insurance Companies)

Area of Planning	Corporate Frequency of Planning by Period (Stated in Years)												
	1	2	3	4	5	6	7	8	9	10	15	20	25
Product Research & Develept			1		1								
Product Costing					1								
Facilities										1			
Manufacturing/Production													
Finance										1			
Credit													
Marketing					2								
Organization Structure					2								
Executive Development					2								
Industrial Relations													
Personnel					2								
Policy Formulation													
Public Relations													
Sources of Raw Materials													
Sources of Supplies													
Subcontracting													
Product Distribution					1								
Charity Contributions													
Product Engineering													
Real Estate													1
Mfg. Methods & Processes										1			
Product Competition													
Advertising	1												
"Size Planning"					1								

TABLE 17

PERIOD OF PLANNING BY SELECTED CORPORATIONS
(Commercial Banks)

Area of Planning	Corporate Frequency of Planning by Period (Stated in Years)												
	1	2	3	4	5	6	7	8	9	10	15	20	25
Product Research & Developt					1								
Product Costing					1								
Facilities			2		2								
Manufacturing/Production													
Finance					3					1			
Credit					1								
Marketing		2			3								
Organizational Structure					1								
Executive Development					1					3			
Industrial Relations					1								
Personnel					2					2			
Policy Formulation					1								
Public Relations		2			2								
Sources of Raw Materials													
Sources of Supplies													
Subcontracting													
Product Distribution													
Charity Contributions													
Product Engineering													
Real Estate			2		2								
Mfg. Methods & Processes					1								
Product Competition	1	2			1								
Advertising	2				2								
"Size Planning"					1								

TABLE 18

PERIOD OF PLANNING BY SELECTED CORPORATIONS
(Merchandising Firms)

Area of Planning	Corporate Frequency of Planning by Period (Stated in Years)												
	1	2	3	4	5	6	7	8	9	10	15	20	25
Product Research & Developt.					2					1			
Product Costing	1	1											
Facilities			1		2	1				2			
Manufacturing/Production	1		1		1					1			
Finance		1	1		1	1				1			
Credit	1												
Marketing		1	1		1	1				1			
Organizational Structure	1		1		2	1							
Executive Development	1				3	1							
Industrial Relations	1	1											
Personnel	1	1			1								
Policy Formulation	1		1										
Public Relations	1	1			1								
Sources of Raw Materials					1								
Sources of Supplies		1											
Subcontracting	1												
Product Distribution					1					1			
Charity Contributions	1												
Product Engineering	1												
Real Estate	1	1								1			
Mfg. Methods & Processes					2					1			
Product Competition	1	1								1			
Advertising	2												
"Size Planning"			1		1			1					

Organizational and Procedural Arrangements for
Long-Range Planning

Contemporary businesses reflect certain organizational postures for effecting long-range planning; they also employ certain tools and plan according to selected procedures; in addition certain dependence on extra-organizational agencies is required. What business contemporaries are doing in this respect is reflected in the following pages.

Organizational Structure for Long-Range Planning

Most of the cooperating companies established a specific organizational entity for long-range planning subsequent to World War II and more especially since 1950. Table 7 reflects the year in which participating companies established a specific organizational entity for long-range planning.[11] There was a noticeable lack of unique organizational units appointed during the depression probably owing to the fact that managers were preoccupied with keeping the organization intact and less concerned with the long-term future. Although the literature of the period 1940-1950 reflected that increasing attention was being given to post-war planning only six companies reported that a specific planning group was established during the period. The majority of the companies organized for long-range planning subsequent to 1950.

The fact that most companies consider long-range planning as a top level management function is evidenced by an analysis of what organizational level the individual in charge of long-range planning is assigned. In this regard Table 19 reflects the organizational level assignment of

-----

[11]See page 125.

the individual in charge of long-range planning. As may be deduced from the examination of the responses to this question, the individual in charge of long-range planning is a top management official. This view is supported by contemporary literature.

TABLE 19

ORGANIZATIONAL ASSIGNMENT LEVEL OF INDIVIDUAL IN CHARGE
OF LONG-RANGE PLANNING

Organizational Level	Frequency Reported
Vice President	37
Comptroller	8
Staff Assistant to President	5
President	5
Chairman of the Board	4
Department Head	4
General Manager	3
Treasurer	3
Reports to President	2
Assist General Manager	2

Before cooperating organizations appointed an organizational entity for long-range planning, the function was performed by various individuals and groups. Ad hoc task groups, executive committees, coordinating committees (composed of financial, marketing, production, research and administrative personnel), product planning officers, and divisional industrial engineering departments are a few of the alternatives offered. Table 20 reflects the responses to the question concerning how and where the long-range planning function was performed prior to the appointment of a specific organizational group.

TABLE 20

AGENCY PERFORMING LONG-RANGE PLANNING BEFORE APPOINTMENT OF
SPECIFIC ORGANIZATIONAL ENTITY

Agency	Frequency of Responses
President or Executive Vice-President	47
Other Top Officer Personnel	31
Board of Directors	15
Financial Officer	15
Marketing-Sales Manager	13
Additional Duty of Key Officer	11

In the majority of responses it is indicated that the president, the executive vice-president, or other top official performed the long-range
planning function--in all probability with assistance from the heads of
the functional departments. An interesting observation is worthy of mention here: contemporary literature indicates that the corporate financial
officer, who worked with long-term financial prognostications before
long-range planning was applied to other corporate areas, was most often
the one who performed the long-range planning apparently because of the
long-term nature of his financial planning. The results of the present
survey do not bear this out as the companies reporting indicate that the
financial officer was not more significantly engaged in long-range planning than other high level executive personnel; in fact three other individuals were more frequently involved. The study also indicates that long-
range planning, even before specific organization groups were created for
the purpose, was a top-level job. It is interesting also to note that
individuals who performed long-range planning were heads of groups representing some of the organic functions of business, viz., distribution and
finance.

Contemporary organizational structures for accomplishing long-range planning vary depending upon the specific problem being analyzed. Many of the companies use a long-range planning office as such as evidenced by Table 21; however, in 30 of the companies long-range planning is assigned as a specific responsibility to a major functional area of effort. One company interviewed indicated that no specific structure existed for long-range planning; rather it was considered every manager's responsibility. In this particular company there was an apparent lack of overall coordinating responsibility for long-range planning. Contemporary literature appears to support the use of a committee for long-range planning. The results of the survey indicate that there is a tendency to move from the use of a committee towards placing long-range plan-

TABLE 21

PRESENT ORGANIZATIONAL STRUCTURE USED TO ACCOMPLISH
LONG-RANGE PLANNING

Type of Structure	Frequency of Use
Assigned as Specific Responsibility to a Major Functional Area of Effort	30
Long-Range Planning Office per se	27
Long-Range Planning Committee	21
"Assistant To" for Long-Range Planning	2

ning responsibility to the functional manager of the area of effort or to a long-range planning office per se. Although contemporary literature does support the idea of a committee for long-range planning there are some writers who question the wisdom of using committees for long-range planning because of the difficulty of fixation of responsibility. Nevertheless it is a means of gaining participation in long-range planning and when used in an advisory capacity can provide yeoman service.

Long-range planning staffs are still relatively small despite the increased attention by managers and management literature to this function. Although the study was concerned with a sampling of the largest corporations in the United States only two companies reported more than 36-72 personnel assigned full time to long-range planning. Table 22 indicates the frequency of use of full time personnel on long-range planning.

TABLE 22

NUMBER OF PERSONNEL ASSIGNED FULL TIME TO THE
LONG-RANGE PLANNING FUNCTION

No. of People	Frequency Reported
1-3	21
3-6	14
6-12	9
18-36	5
12-18	3
36-72	2

The number of personnel assigned full time on long-range planning is relatively easy to determine; however, it is more difficult to identify the number who are assigned to this function part time inasmuch as many companies report that long-range planning is performed as an additional duty of executive personnel. In addition even planning personnel devote only a portion of their time to long-range planning; the remaining time being expended on short-range planning. Various numbers of personnel are reported, as reflected in Table 23, as having part-time long-term planning responsibilities; numbers from one to three hundred are cited; the difficulty of estimating such figures casts some doubt as to the validity and reliability of such reports.

TABLE 23

NUMBER OF PERSONNEL ASSIGNED WHO SPEND MAJOR PART OF
TIME IN LONG-RANGE PLANNING

No. of People	Frequency Reported
1	2
2	1
3	4
4	1
5	4
6	2
10	5
12	1
15	2
18	1
93	1
200 plus	2

The composition of long-range planning staffs by professional areas
of effort reflect a breadth and depth of technical capability. Table 24
indicates the professional areas of effort as reported by respondents.

TABLE 24

PROFESSIONAL AREAS OF EFFORT REPRESENTED
ON LONG-RANGE PLANNING STAFF

Area of Effort	Frequency of Response
Marketing	45
Technical (Engineering)	42
Economics	41
Management	41
Statistics	33
Finance (including Accounting)	31
Production	21
Legal	10
Personnel	8
Real Estate	4
Medical	1

Marketing, technical, economics, and management representation is reported
most frequently. The one company reporting a doctor assigned was a large
drug manufacturing concern.

Participation in the formulation of long-range plans is considered by most scholars as necessary to the successful accomplishment of long-term objectives. In formulating a question to measure how far down the organizational hierarchy participation was required the author endeavored to construct a question which would require the individual answering the question to commit himself specifically.[12] The selection of the typical positions provided some problems, as the echelon titles are peculiar to the particular type of business involved; hence somewhat stereotyped titles were used. Table 25 gives an indication as to how far down the organizational hierarchy participation in long-range planning is required; answers to this question seem to indicate that participation in long-range planning is encouraged at all executive management levels; however, the absence of answers to this question by many companies would indicate that

TABLE 25

DEPTH OF LONG-RANGE PLANNING BY ORGANIZATIONAL HIERARCHY

Organizational Level	Frequency of Response
Through Executive Vice-President	16
Through Vice-President for Functional Area of Effort	29
Through General Manager	32
Through Superintendent	12
Through General Foreman	4
Through Department Chiefs	20
Through Section Chiefs	13

there is some doubt as to just how far the long-range planning participation is carried. One company interviewed reported that participation was carried to the individual workers; another indicated that long-range plan-

---

[12]To simply have asked the question: "Do you require long-range planning participation throughout the organizational structure?" or some such verbage would probably have elicited a yes answer in most cases as this is the answer that would have been expected.

ning was restricted to top management personnel to include product sales
and research and development managers.

The Use of Extra-Organizational Agencies in Long-Range Planning

The provisioning of economic data in the absence of a staff or of
professional economists is accomplished as reflected in Table 26. In one
company interviewed the long-range planning office of the parent company
provided the necessary information to subordinate echelons. Major reliance
is placed on subscribing to outside economic advisory services as well as
perusal by company executives of trade publications, newspapers, periodicals, government publications, and similar media. Two companies, although
claiming engagement in long-range planning, made no special effort to follow current economic conditions.

TABLE 26

METHOD OF OBTAINING ECONOMIC DATA
FOR LONG-RANGE PLANNING

Method	Frequency of Use Reported
Subscribe to Outside Economic Advisory Services	38
Perusal by Company Executives of Trade Publications, Newspapers, Periodicals, Govt. Publications, etc.	35
Provided by Trade Associations	26
Attendance at Professional Meetings	24
Part-time Duty of Specific Company Executive	19
Retain Professional Economist	10
Hire Economist on ad hoc Basis	9
University Contracts	7
No Specific Effort Made to Follow Current Economic Conditions	2

Companies who seek assistance and/or information from outside
agencies report receipt of information or assistance as summarized in
Table 27.

TABLE 27

TYPE OF ASSISTANCE/INFORMATION USED FROM
OUTSIDE CONSULTANT AGENCIES

Type of Information or Assistance	Frequency of Use Reported
Economic Predictions	44
Economic Indicators	41
Gross National Product Statistics	33
Legislative and Technological Evaluations	30
Census of Business Data	20
Statistical Summaries	17
Census of Manufactures' Data	16

Although contemporary management literature reports unfavorably
on the use of management consultants to do all of a company's long-range
planning, 42 companies report the use of such agencies to provide specific
information relative to long-range planning and 36 companies report non-
use. Thirteen companies report they use management consultants to do
their long-range planning while 66 indicate non-use of management consultants for long-range planning.

There has been a decrease in the number of companies using management consultants to effect long-range planning. Twenty-nine companies
report "ever having used" management consultants to do long-range planning, while 48 claim never to have used management consultants.

The reasons for using management consultants to effect long-range
planning as reported by the respondents is indicated in Table 28; this
response indicates that the main reason for seeking outside accomplishment
of the long-range planning is lack of qualified company personnel and the

need for an "outside" evaluation of the long-range planning problem. As
contemporary businesses become more knowledgeable in long-range planning,
it could be expected that the number depending on outside agencies to do
their long-range planning will decrease.

TABLE 28

REASONS FOR USING MANAGEMENT CONSULTANTS TO
EFFECT LONG-RANGE PLANNING

Reason	Frequency of Response
Lack of Qualified Company Personnel	5
Need for an "Outside" Evaluation	4
Workload in Company Precludes Internal Accomplishment of Long-Range Planning	1
Used for Only ad hoc Long-Range Planning Projects	1

Note: Three companies reporting the use of management consultants
to effect long-range planning failed to provide any reason for so doing
rather than accomplishing long-range planning using company resources.

The principal objection to the use of a consultant to do long-
range planning is that the consultant does not have the intimate knowledge of company product, market, organization, personnel capabilities
required to accomplish an effective job of planning. Table 29 reflects
the objections given by select companies. Another objection voiced is
that the consultant is no better equipped than internal company personnel to do long-range planning; five companies claim that long-range planning is a key management responsibility which cannot be delegated. One
company interviewed reported:

> The principal reason that the company does not use a management
> consultant is the view that only by a close and intimate working
> knowledge of the company on a continuing basis, together with a
> close association with the operating line management, can the
> long-range planning function be performed effectively. An out-
> side management consultant might prove helpful in the conduct of
> a specific and precisely defined outside investigation and the com-
> pany is not adverse to using such services under these circumstances.

There should be no real objection to using management consultants for specialized assistance in long-range planning. Consultants can provide a refreshing new look at a proposal and provide specific types of data not economically obtainable by the company staff or for use on specific projects where the consultants can devote time to the project which is not readily obtainable within the company.

TABLE 29

OBJECTIONS GIVEN BY SELECT COMPANIES TO USING MANAGEMENT CONSULTANT TO
ACCOMPLISH ALL OR A MAJOR PART OF CORPORATE LONG-RANGE PLANNING

Reason	Frequency Reported
Consultant does not have intimate knowledge of company product, market, organization, personnel capabilities	22
No better equipped than internal company people to do long-range planning	8
Long-range planning is a key management responsibility and cannot be delegated	5
Time required by consultants to effect corporate long-range planning	4
Importance of long-range planning dictates it be accomplished internally	3
Too costly	3
Lack of realism on part of the consultant	2
Use of consultant does not improve skills of company planners	2
Company personnel have done better job than consultants used	2
Consultant unable to follow up as can company people	1
"By-products" of planning lost if outside agencies do long-range planning	1

Note: The question concerning the above required a narrative answer from the respondents on the questionnaire. The above structure of answers has been formulated based on the author's classification of the responses; in many cases the answers did not follow the above verbage but it was the author's opinion that the main intent of the answer fell into an appropriate category as reflected above.

The Tools of Long-Range Planning

Tools of long-range planning are the functional and other devices
that are employed by planners to assist in the identification and interpretation of significant data relative to long-range planning. Some of
these tools are classical in the sense that they have been employed in
business activities since antiquity in one form or another; others are
of more recent innovation and in some cases still in developmental stages.
Table 30 reflects the tools that are used by contemporary businesses in
their long-range planning deliberations.

TABLE 30

TOOLS EMPLOYED BY SELECT CORPORATIONS IN EFFECTING
LONG-RANGE PLANNING

Type of Tool	Frequency of Use Reported
Budgets	69
Statistical Analysis and Inference	66
Financial Statements	65
Correlation and Trend Analysis	59
Break-Even Charts	37
Operations Research	29
Linear Programming	21
Mathematical Models	20
Operational Models	11
Input-Output Theory	10
Game Theory	9
Ecological Models	1

While newer techniques and tools are continually being tested and in
some cases applied with good results, most problems relative to long-
range planning are still being handled with the more traditional and
basic tools. Budgets, financial statements, and statistical analysis/
inference are reported most frequently as tools of long-range planning.
Correlation and trend analysis, operations research, and break-even

charts are reported with significant frequency. Ecological models, as a tool of long-range planning, have been suggested by contemporary literature but only one company in the survey reported the use of such a model.[13]

Tools used in long-range planning are still the traditional ones which have been highly developed in other phases of the business organization. As the state of the art advances in long-range planning it is expected that a greater use will be made of some of the newer tools such as game theory, operational models, input-output theory, and others. For many companies the immediate problems seem to be those of setting up a basic long-range planning capability using the known and understood basic tools; as the company becomes more familiar with long-term planning methods doubtlessly more advanced procedures and techniques will be explored.

The use of these tools does not, in any sense of the word, negate the requirement for the exercise of executive judgment in the long-range planning process. Executive reflective thinking and the mental balancing of the pros and cons of a long-term decision still must be effected by the executive regardless of the degree of refinement of his planning tools.

The Accomplishment of Long-Range Planning

Once organizational and procedural arrangements for long-range planning are established the company must face the actual accomplishment of long-range planning; objectives must be established, planning by func-

---

[13]Platt & Maines, op. cit., pp. 125-126.

tional area identified, limitations and difficulties corrected, plans coordinated, and the mechanics of review developed. Then too, the executive group will doubtlessly elect to "pretest" its long-range planning and develop forecasting techniques. The effect of extra-organizational factors must be taken into consideration; finally the results of long-range planning remain to be evaluated to determine if the product of the planning was worth the investment. The next few pages examine how contemporary business organizations accomplish their long-range planning with respect to the above areas.

The Establishment of Objectives for Long-Range Planning

The problem of setting necessary objectives for long-range planning is a fundamental task for management. Objectives that are established should be realistic, attainable, and compatible with the organizational service objective. Research seems to be a basic part of setting long-term objectives; objectives arise from preliminary planning studies. General objectives may be formulated by top management which are couched in such broad terms as to be applicable to the entire business. A danger here is that general objectives may be so all-encompassing and comprehensive that subordinate executive personnel have difficulty in identifying themselves or their unit with the objective.

A basic question arises from the foregoing, viz., are long-range goals and/or objectives set before the long-range planning process is initiated or do the objectives grow out of such planning. Table 31 represents the policy of contemporary businesses for establishing long-range planning objectives. Corporate objectives grow out of long-range planning in the majority of the cases reported although a substantial number of companies report that objectives are established before the long-range planning is effected. Three companies report that their objectives are established without any long-range planning activities either before or after the objective setting. In all probability all companies enter into some form of long-range planning before establishing long-term objectives. Even though a substantial portion claim to establish objectives before entering into long-range planning, doubtlessly the corporation president or the board of directors has had a mental plan or image against which to test the long-term objective for feasibility, compatibility, and attainability. To suppose that far-future objectives can be established without some sort of long-range planning is believed faulty reasoning. How else can the company determine how and where it wants to go?

TABLE 31

POLICY FOR ESTABLISHING LONG-RANGE PLANNING OBJECTIVES

Procedure for Establish- ing Objectives	Frequency Method Reported
Objectives Grow out of Long-Range Planning	57
Objectives Established before Long-Range Planning	29
Board of Directors sets Objectives upon which Long-Range Planning is Predicated	6
Objectives Established without Long-Range Planning Activities	3

The objective setting should be limited to major areas of consideration and should start with a careful study of the industry environment as a basis for appraising the company's position and its strengths and limitations. Out of this should grow preliminary planning and the final establishment of objectives against which long-range planning is directed.

The Pretesting of Long-Range Plans

Once the lengthy process of developing a plan is completed, what assurance does management have that the plan is going to operate as envisioned by the framers? Several alternative methods exist for determining the success of a plan after it has been consummated and implemented. The acid test for the entire forward plan is return on investment in quantitative terms and in the degree of accomplishment of the organizational service objective. This method of testing, however, is impracticable for the company which desires to evaluate and predict the success of its pending long-range plans. As the plan is developed each sub-plan and every facet of supporting data have probably been subjected to executive judgment of one sort or another before integration into the master plan. The testing of the sub-plan does not, however, negate the requirement for some form of pretesting on the integrated package plan. Any waiting for the pragmatic test of history is unacceptable if timely improvement of long-range planning techniques and process is to be effected.

The techniques reported by industry to pretest its plans vary from the use of formal decision laboratories where computers and models are used to the informal "mental testing" done by a manager when he approves a definite step or approach in the formulation of a plan. As Table 32 indicates the principal method thus far and the one which seems to pervade all areas, is management judgment. There appears to be no single or uniform technique; yet the methods reported reflect a broad approach to this activity. The low response made by the respondents to the question concerning the method used to test long-range plans seems to indicate that much development needs to be accomplished by industry in or-

der to refine this sphere of activity. Companies as a group do not indicate that a high degree of attempts at testing long-range planning has
been developed.

TABLE 32

METHODS USED BY CORPORATIONS TO PRETEST LONG-RANGE PLANNING

Method of Testing	Reported Frequency of Use
Executive Judgment	63
Operations Research	18
Executive Seminars	17
Computer Techniques	16
Mathematical Models	15
Coordination with Management Consultant Agencies	11
Operational Models	10
No attempt to Pretest	3
"Business Games"	2
Ecological Models	1

Contemporary literature is almost devoid of writings on the subject
of pretesting long-range plans. Only one article treating with this subject to any depth was located by the author.[14] Seven companies specifically noted their "weakness" in this area and stated that they plan to
develop this technique as part of their plans for future refinement of
long-range planning.

There are not now any all-encompassing models in operations research
that can be relied on to evaluate over-all company long-range planning.
Some techniques exist which can enable a company to perform an elementary
test of its activities in the realm of long-term planning. Techniques

---

[14]See William J. Platt and N. Robert Maines, "Pretest Your Long-
Range Plans," Harvard Business Review (January-February, 1959), p. 119.

of rolling forecasts and overlapping plans tends to result in pretesting
by executive judgment. The use of computer experimentation, business
games, and such tools should yield valuable test reports that can direct
management toward better long-range plans. Much creative work needs to
be done to develop valid techniques to accomplish this testing. Any innovation developed in the future will remain, however, essentially a
tool, inasmuch as the final pretest of a plan rests on the judgment of
the responsible executive; the final test is one of progmatic results.

The Functional Areas of Long-Range Planning

Cooperating companies indicate that in general there are few
functions which are not subject to planning on a long-term basis. Not
every field of activity is planned in every company; even in companies
in the same general classification by type such as industrials, there
are differences in the period for which long-range plans are formulated.[15]
Table 33 reflects the functional and other areas of effort where long-
range planning is reported by cooperating companies. In the questionnaire respondents were requested to indicate the five most critical
areas of long-range planning as pertains to their company. In this
respect the organic functions of business are included in the five most
critical areas of planning; it appears that the emphasis placed on long-
range planning varies according to the significance of the different activities in each corporation's overall operations. Ancillary functions,
that is functions which support major functions in the business, appear
of less importance in the long-range planning process but nevertheless
are subjected to the long-term approach.

_____

[15]See pp. 133-141 for a discussion of the period of planning by
functional area of effort.

TABLE 33

FUNCTIONAL AND OTHER AREAS OF EFFORT WHERE LONG-RANGE PLANNING IS
REPORTED BY COOPERATING COMPANIES

Corporate Area of Effort	Frequency Reported	Frequency Reported as One of Five Most Critical Areas
Marketing	57	52
Facilities	50	38
Finance	50	36
Product Research and Development	48	44
Product Competition	38	21
Manufacturing/Production	36	24
Organizational Structure	32	9
Personnel	31	17
Product Distribution	28	6
"Size Planning," i.e., develop long-term objectives as to how large your business should be	28	16
Manufacturing Methods and Processes	26	14
Product Costing	25	10
Product Engineering	25	13
Policy Formulation	24	9
Executive Development	23	9
Sources of Raw Materials	21	11
Industrial Relations	17	6
Sources of Supplies	17	2
Real Estate	17	7
Credit	15	2
Public Relations	15	1
Subcontracting	14	1
Advertising	14	3
Charity Contributions	5	0

Difficulties and Limitations of Long-Range Planning

Though 86 per cent of the cooperating businesses report that they are actively engaged in long-range planning activities, this functional area of effort is not without difficulties and limitations. Table 34 reflects the difficulties and limitations of long-range planning as reported by selected companies; the table also shows the frequency that the difficulty or limitation was reported by order of importance by the respondents. Lack of accurate data, development of adequate forecasting techniques, preoccupation of management on immediate operating problems, and the establishment of suitable long-range objectives predominate as the major difficulties and limitations. With the exception of the lack of accurate data other major difficulties and limitations of long-range are attributable to factors, forces, and activities which are within the jurisdiction of the corporate management. The second, third, fourth, and fifth most frequently reported difficulties (preoccupation of management on immediate operating problems, forecasting techniques, establishing long-range objectives, and effecting intra-company coordination of long-range planning activities) and other difficulties are all matters which, in the main, can be refined and corrected through internal management practices. Lack of accurate data (external data), business cycle influences, government controls, and industry peculiarities although reported as a difficulty or limitation are beyond the jurisdiction of corporate management and as such must be accepted as influencing the long-range planning without any direct control thereof by the corporation.

Extra-organizational difficulties, such as governmental controls, business cycle influences, and industry peculiarities, play a relatively

TABLE 34

DIFFICULTIES AND LIMITATIONS OF LONG-RANGE PLANNING AS
REPORTED BY SELECT COMPANIES

Difficulty or Limitation	Frequency Reported	Frequency that Difficulty or Limitation was Reported by Order of Importance					
		1st	2nd	3rd	4th	5th	6th
Forecasting Techniques	46	6	10	6	5	3	3
Lack of Accurate Data	45	18	6	4	5	2	
Preoccupation of Management on Immediate Operating Problems	45	11	10	6	1	3	
Establishing Long-Range Objectives	35	4	3	9	2	1	5
Effecting Intra-Company Coordination of LRP Activities	29	4	0	9	3	2	1
Personnel Limitations	28	3	9	1	2		2
Having Suitable Organizational Structure to Effect LRP	24	2	4	3	2	1	2
Establishing LRP Policies, Procedures, Techniques	22	2	5	3	5	2	1
Government Controls	22	2	3	5	3	5	2
Reviewing, Revising and Updating LRP	20	1	0	4	3	2	1
Industry Peculiarities	18	5	1	3	1	1	2
Gaining Wholehearted Top Management Support	14	1	6	1	2	3	
Business Cycle Influences	14	3	3	2	1	1	
Getting Middle Management Support	2						
No Difficulties or Limitations	2						

minor role. This suggests that the refinement of a company's long-range
planning function is well within the jurisdiction of the management
group and can be improved by internal organization, policies, and procedures. In all probability these difficulties and limitations will dimin-
ish in importance as American management becomes more astute in the area
of long-range planning; inasmuch as long-range planning is a relatively
recent innovation in business, it is to be expected that there will be
sophistication and further development of long-range planning techniques.
It is believed that all of the difficulties listed on Table 34 are encountered in one phase or another in any long-range planning activity.
Their relative importance varies depending upon particular circumstances
and the time period under consideration; for many organizations it is
difficult to generalize on the relative importance of the difficulties.
Other considerations unfavorable to long-range planning are elements
which are related to management attitudes and include overt or passive
resistance to the planner's work by such tactics as the withholding of
vital information and the subtle resisting of change or of the frank consideration of measures for improvement. Other attitudes are these:

> Misconceptions about the nature of corporate planning and the plan-
> ner's authority; unwillingness to be tied to a commitment that
> seems to preclude further deliberation; fear of being controlled
> by planners or unsympathetic outsiders; resistance to ideas intro-
> duced by others; professional jealousy and factional narrowness;
> undue preoccupation with the present and too much motivation from
> short-run incentives; natural complacency over past success which
> came without benefit of planning.[16]

---

[16]The Corporate Planner and His Job, Report No. 125 (Menlo Park,
California: Stanford Research Institute, January 1962).

Overcoming Difficulties and Limitations

The long-range planning process is evolving and developing. Difficulties and limitations experienced have only been those normally expected in the development of a new concept. In the study cooperating organizations were requested to relate how they had attempted to overcome the difficulties and limitations of planning. Responses to this question were disappointing; in fact only 15 companies related their experience and intentions in this area. The responses were so few and heterogeneous in nature that any quantification was impossible; consequently methods and techniques used to overcome difficulties and limitations will be reflected in qualitative terms.

Techniques employed to overcome the difficulties and limitations of planning depend of course upon the particular difficulty encountered. Conducting briefings on long-range planning is one method cited. The preparation of more detailed justifications in support of various tasks of research and development programs, lending increased validity to selected areas of study and development, also facilitates the planning process. The task of continuously re-examining future plans, of comparing results with plans and of encouraging creative and reflective thinking among executive personnel represent other management improvement areas in long-range planning.

Lack of accurate data as a difficulty is correctable to a degree through the study of existing periodical and book literature; in addition, the perusal of government statistics provides a prolific source of data needed for long-range planning. Piecing together of market intelligence requires ingenuity to solicit and seek data from a wide range of sources and to attempt to discern a pattern that might emerge from an evaluation of such data as are available. In speaking of mitigating the

problem of lack of accurate data one large aircraft manufacturer said:

> In addition to the intelligence sources of the operating divisions
> and the corporate office, use is made of the district offices who
> are in close contact with representatives of the customer. We al-
> so attempt to use industry association data and published financial
> reports of competitors.

As would be expected one of the most frequent methods reported for

overcoming long-range planning difficulties is to improve the capabilities

and capacities of personnel engaged in planning. This is accomplished

through a variety of means such as requiring frequent meetings between

planners and heads of the operating department; by improving planning

procedures and aiding company personnel in their understanding of such

procedures; by requiring the maximum participation in the planning pro-

cess; by rotating the planners and the operating heads into the long-

range planning staff positions; and by other personnel development pro-

grams. Other singular means used to overcome difficulties, as related

to specific problems are reported:

> Since our long-range planning or Corporate Planning Department,
> as we describe it, is relatively new, we have had the greatest
> effect in effecting intracompany coordination of long-range plan-
> ning activities through personal contact between the Corporate
> Planning Group and the Operating Division heads responsible for
> divisional long-range planning. The enlargement of the budget-
> ing technique to include not only expense and capital assets bud-
> get for the coming fiscal year but five-year projections into the
> future for both expense and capital assets budgets has provided
> a broader base for consolidation and consideration on a total cor-
> porate basis.
>
> Increasing skill in the development of sources of data and fore-
> casting techniques has come from careful attention to the litera-
> ture on both subjects and expanding experience of the individual
> executives involved. Some sharpening of abilities in this field
> has come from the experience in acquisitions and analysis of pos-
> sible acquisitions, as well as management training programs or
> outside seminars, such as those conducted by AMA.

A combination of all of the above, including regular revision and review of long-range plans has been so far most effective in overcoming the pre-occupation of operating management on immediate operating problems. This area has also been further improved by the recently instituted Operating Division and Corporate Division executive conferences now being held once every six months, during which time considerable attention is given to long-range planning and its various functional areas.

Other reasons exist to cause plans to fail; lack of support from top management, undue separation of planning from operations, failure to put plans in writing, and failure to make timely decisions are but a few which may be cited. Notwithstanding the existence of such possible contingencies participating American businesses have developed a high degree of participation in planning which seems to indicate that most of the difficulties and limitations involved in the long-range process have been largely overcome.

Extra-Organizational Factors Affecting Long-Range Planning

Extra-organizational factors play an important role in the development of meaningful plans for a company's future. Any firm which establishes long-range plans, whether they be expressed in terms of volume, of capital outlay programs, of profits, of service, or of new products, is likely to find many variables which should be reviewed from the company's external environment. Business is affected intimately by a great many factors beyond its control such as the general level of prosperity in the country, access to foreign markets, tariff protection against imports, general availability of money for capital, government controls and other factors which must be identified and evaluated as part of the long-range planning. External factors are not just related to the general economy and the individual company's position in the market; they should also include a careful appraisal of what competitors are doing with their product lines, prices, distribution methods and their long-range planning.

Contemporary businesses consider a broad base of economic phenomena composed of complex external factors and forces. Table 35 reflects the external factors that are considered by the respondent businesses in their long-range planning activities.

TABLE 35

EXTERNAL FACTORS CONSIDERED IN LONG-RANGE PLANNING ACTIVITIES
OF SELECT CORPORATIONS

Factor of Consideration	Frequency Reported
Industry Trends	69
Competitors' Actions	67
Technological Progress	63
Population Factors	55
Legislative Actions	51
Business Cycles	49
Government National Product Changes	47
Government Controls	46
Government Expenditures	44
International Matters	43
Government Fiscal Policy	43
Political Environment	36
New Construction	29
Employment	23
Housing Statistics	22
Social Mores	10
Fashion and Styles	7

As may be noted from the table competitors' actions and industry trends are cited most frequently as a consideration of long-range planning. Technological progress, population factors, and legislative actions are also frequently reported. Government expenditures and controls are of prime importance in the planning activity of defense contractors; companies engaged in producing consumer goods paid more attention to population factors than did the producer goods manufacturers. As far as the firm's industry was concerned respondents report that they attempt to evaluate their competitive position as well as the growth and decline trends of the parent industry. Table 36 represents the key influences or factors in an industry which cooperating organizations attempt to evaluate. Another prime factor of consideration is the overall competitive position of the industry as well as the industry demand. Thirty-five companies report that they make an attempt to evaluate the long-range planning techniques of competitors in the industry.

TABLE 36

KEY INFLUENCES OR FACTORS IN COMPANY INDUSTRY EVALUATED BY
SELECT CORPORATIONS

Factor	Frequency Reported
Growth/Decline Trends	74
Competitive Position	73
Individual Firm's Position	66
Industry Demands	63
Long-Range Planning Techniques	35

Evaluation of the long-range planning techniques of competitors is accomplished in a variety of ways. Inasmuch as most firms guard closely their long-range planning documents and techniques this becomes a formidable task. Table 37 represents the methods reported by companies used to evaluate long-range planning techniques and results of their industry. Although 34 reported that they make an attempt to evaluate the long-range planning techniques of their industry only 29 companies cited the methods used.[17]

TABLE 37

METHOD REPORTED BY COMPANIES USED TO EVALUATE LONG-RANGE PLANNING
TECHNIQUES AND RESULTS OF THEIR INDUSTRY

Method Reported	Frequency Reported
Through examination of key decisions of competitors vs apparent direction and payoff of these decisions	8
Judgment of planners based on informal visits and discussions	7
Trade association contacts	6
Statistical studies	4
Published reports of competitors, e.g., annual reports	2
Through use of published government data	1
Company executive seminars	1

An integral part of evaluating the influencing factors in the industry is the identification and integration of customer viewpoint and data into long-range planning deliberations. Sixty-two of the respondents indicate that an attempt is made to bring in the customer's viewpoint; six companies report no attempt is made to reflect customer viewpoint in long-range planning deliberations. One company interviewed had developed a special staff agency to accomplish this; in others it appears to be provided through a combination of a formal staff agency and/or through the informal procedures and structure of the sales executive

---

[17]The author classified the various methods reported by respondents into the above table. Low response to this question and the variety of answers precluded any precise quantification of the response; the above categorization is based on the author's best judgment as to the general classification of the method or technique.

staff and from information obtained from salesmen or technical representative field contacts. Table 38 represents the author's classification of the methods used by respondents for integration of customer viewpoint in the long-range plans.

TABLE 38

MECHANICS OF HOW COMPANIES INTEGRATE CUSTOMER VIEWPOINT AND
INFLUENCES INTO INTERNAL LONG-RANGE PLANNING DELIBERATIONS

Method Reported	Frequency Reported
Marketing Research Activity	18
Feedback from Sales Department	10
Executive Judgment	10
Specific Customer Surveys	9
Continual Contact with Customer by Executive Personnel	5
Personal Interview with Key Customers	4
No Formal Method Exists; Done on Informal Basis	4
Through Study of Trade Association Marketing Data	2

Trade associations appear to play an important part in providing information and assistance to companies engaged in long-range planning. In this respect 46 of the respondents indicate that trade associations provide information and assistance; 26 claim to receive no assistance from trade associations.

Another source of economic data and information concerning market
potential and other factors of the economy is through the utilization of
published source material. Table 39 reflects the frequency of use of
published source material for long-range planning.

TABLE 39

FREQUENCY OF USE OF PUBLISHED SOURCE MATERIAL
FOR LONG-RANGE PLANNING

Source Material	Frequency of Use Reported
Government Statistics	75
Commerce Department Reports	61
Trade Association Data	60
Periodicals	58
Books	48
AMA Special Reports	44
University Business Research Reports	43

The foregoing suggests that an integral part of the long-range planning
staff should be an information collection agency organized along the lines
of the intelligence office of a military general staff. Such an effort
could be provided to collect raw intelligence information, interpret it,
and disseminate it for the use and guidance of collateral staff agencies
engaged in planning. Although the military general staff intelligence
effort is of greater magnitude than such an activity would be even in a
large corporation, the fundamental concept is still applicable.

Forecasting in Long-Range Planning

Drucker defines long-range planning by what it is not rather than by what it is. First, ". . . it is not forecasting. It is not master-minding the future, . . . long-range planning is necessary precisely because we cannot forecast."[18] Forecasting attempts to find the most probable course of events or at best a range of probabilities by assessing future environments and the mutual impact of such environments on the organization and the organization on the environments. Planning occurs at a later date when the company evaluates the forecast information and converts it into objectives, plans, policies, programs, and procedures which guide the corporate action.

Forecasts are developed based on both internal and external data; the latter are more involved and less predictable. Table 40 reflects the internal company data used for forecasting and long-range planning as reported by the respondents in the study.

TABLE 40

INTERNAL COMPANY DATA USED IN COMPANY LONG-RANGE PLANNING

Type of Data	Frequency of Use Reported
Sales Forecasts	76
Present Sales Data	71
Financial Data	66
Cost Data	62
Product Data	55
Personnel Data	50
Manufacturing Techniques	50
Plant and Equipment Maturity Data	47
Personnel Capabilities	46
Organization Posture	35
Labor Availability	29
Credit Data	15

As may be noted from the table sales forecasts and present sales data are frequently made and used in company long-range planning; cost and financial data also play an important part in a company's forecasting procedures.

External data and specific forecasts effected relative to long-range planning as reported by the respondents in Table 41 reflect a broad spectrum of forecasts, ranging from sales forecasts to attempts at predicting the social mores of certain customers.

TABLE 41

FORECASTS EFFECTED RELATIVE TO LONG-RANGE PLANNING
AS REPORTED BY RESPONDENTS

Type of Forecast	Frequency Reported
Sales	74
Industry Trends	68
Profit	67
Share of Market	66
Total Customer Potential	63
Costs	55
Prices	53
Product Diversification	52
Population Trends	51
Technological Progress	51
Gross National Product Changes	48
Government Expenditures	45
Capital Availability	44
Product Life	44
Employment Requirements	38
New Construction	36
International Conditions	36
Marketing	36
Consumer Buying Power	34
Raw Material Prices	30
Political Environment	29
Legislative	24
Standard of Living Progression	24
Social Mores	10

The degree of participation by cooperating companies in forecasting seems to indicate that considerable management attention has been paid to this activity. The breadth of functional and other areas of long-range planning which has been facilitated by forecasting indicates that this will continue to be an import area. Complex factors and forces affecting the company dictate that a company engaged in long-range planning must develop comprehensive and accurate forecasting techniques.

The Results of Long-Range Planning

The most valuable result of long-range planning stems from the fact that business is better prepared to meet the uncertain future and to assume the right risks necessary to survive in the competitive environment; "crisis management" becomes less pronounced and short term dips in the economy become less significant. The results of long-range planning are manifested in direct as well as indirect ways; the present chapter is concerned with the direct results as reported by respondents in the study.

TABLE 42

ORGANIZATIONAL, PRODUCT, AND OTHER CHANGES RESULTING DIRECTLY FROM
LONG-RANGE PLANNING AS REPORTED BY RESPONDENT COMPANIES

Change Reported	Frequency Reported
New Product Lines	39
Product Diversification	38
Company Acquisitions	36
Executive Development Program	26
Company Reorganizations	26
Organizational Decentralization	18
Company Mergers	16
No Changes	13

Table 42 summarizes the organizational, product, and other changes resulting directly from long-range planning as reported by respondent com-

panies. The most frequently reported results have been the development
of new product lines and product diversifications. Long-range planning
has played a significant role in company acquisitions; 45 per cent of
the respondents report acquisitions as a direct result of long-range
planning; 34 per cent of the respondents have effected company reorganizations as a result of long-range planning. Thirteen companies indicate no organizational or product changes have resulted from the long-
range planning activity; this is attributable in the main to the fact
that only recently have these companies established a long-range planning effort and insufficient time has elapsed to see any results.

Another result of the long-range planning deliberations is the
creation of "planning documents" created to implement the long-term
plans. Table 43 summarizes the planning documents created as a result
of long-range planning in the respondent companies.

TABLE 43

PLANNING DOCUMENTS CREATED AS RESULT OF LONG-RANGE PLANNING
IN COOPERATING COMPANIES

Planning Document Reported	Frequency Reported
Long-range plan for specific segments of the company	45
"Master" plan for future	39
Functional area long-range plans	37
Economic predictions	36

The creation of a specific long-range plan for certain segments of the
company is reported most frequently. The development of functional area
long-range plans is reported in slightly less than half of the companies.

The long-range plan is the most obvious result of the long-range
planning process. After a plan has been developed and accepted by the

board of directors, the question arises as to how it will be communicated to those responsible for implementing it. Several alternative methods are reported by companies studied, as reflected in Table 44. The greater portion of the companies responding favorably to this question report the use of intra-company briefings to communicate the long-range plan; integration of the plans into a master plan and then distributing to all echelons responsible for implementing a portion of the master plan is reported in 15 of the companies. Other singular methods reported in addition to those reflected in the table for communicating the plans are shown below.

TABLE 44

METHOD OF "COMMUNICATING" LONG-RANGE PLANNING AFTER IT HAS
BEEN DEVELOPED AND ACCEPTED

Method Reported	Frequency Reported
Use intra-company briefings	23
Limited distribution of "master plan"	15
Use company seminars	14
Distribute functional area long-range plans only; no attempt made to distribute master plan	13
Integrated into master plan and distributed to line managers	12
Integrate into master plan and distribute to all echelons responsible for implementing a portion of master plan	12
No distribution effected; line managers responsible for implementing own long-range plans and for company coordination thereof	4

1. Continuous education through personal contacts of executive personnel.

2. Long-range plans are developed, reviewed and integrated at each major level in the corporation beginning with major function and project elements of the division, the division as a whole, and the cor-

poration as a whole. Assistance is provided by planning staffs appropriate to each area of activity. Approvals of long-range planning are principally in the form of authorizations and approvals relating to implementing decisions which are communicated to the responsible organizations.

3. Planning is on a continuous basis with coordination with affected operating and engineering departments during the development of plans and the distribution of the results of planning.

4. Master plan has limited distribution to the board of directors, president and group vice-presidents. Operating sections of the master plan are distributed to various division managers.

5. Implementation is triggered by an "action" directive from the president.

6. For two companies the "master plan" is given a limited distribution:

    a. To the board of directors, key officers and major department heads.

    b. To divisional and major department heads.

    c. At ad hoc management meetings to key executives.

In one company interviewed all concerned individuals are provided with such information, developed through long-range planning, as may be useful or helpful to them in their work. Long-range plans are generally communicated to those responsible for implementing them through the line management organization. However, the echelon levels to which plans are distributed indicate that some of the lower level managers do not actually receive copies of the master plan but rather receive operating instructions drawn from the master long-range plan. Thus, each subordinate is informed by his superior as to the goals he is asked to strive toward, and performance is reviewed by his superior. Usually the individuals involved have already contributed to the formulation of the plans.

The Coordination and Review of Long-Range Planning

Coordination involves the synchronizing of related activities with respect to the time and order of performance; the method of achieving coordination is largely horizontal although it does involve the relating of vertical activities. Coordination of the long-range planning deliberations may be accomplished through several formal and informal techniques. Probably the most frequently used method of coordination is that effected by individual executives as required to develop their input into the planning.

Table 45 reflects the internal policies and procedures used for coordinating long-range planning activities in the sample companies.

TABLE 45

INTERNAL POLICIES AND PROCEDURES USED FOR COORDINATING
LONG-RANGE PLANNING ACTIVITIES

Method of Obtaining Coordination	Frequency Reported
Normal intrastaff coordination	49
Ad hoc coordination	28
Standing planning committee	25
Board of directors	15
Intra-company routing of plan	14
Departmental seminar	13

Normal intra-staff coordination predominates as the method for effecting the coordination of long-term planning. One company interviewed, which operated in a decentralized environment, reported that the operating divisions develop long-range divisional plans in which the plans for functional departments are integrated. Coordination of the divisional plans into the corporate long-range plans is accomplished in several steps; a typical step is achieved through review and approval of capital assets budget; another through review and coordination of research and development budgets; a third is through review and semi-annual revision of comprehensive financial forecasts and plans. During the review process there is normal intra-staff coordination and then after approval of the basic budgets, intra-company routing of the resultant sectors of the master plan. The long-range planning activities relating to a single department are coordinated by that department. If it concerns two departments or more, initially the heads of the departments will attempt to coordinate and resolve the problem areas if it cannot be accomplished by subordinate personnel; and so the coordinating process continues up through the managerial hierarchy with final coordination effected by the executive planning committee or comparable level organizational element. Another company reported its coordination activity:

> Long-range plans are developed, reviewed and integrated at each major level in the corporation, beginning with major functional and project elements of the division, the division as a whole, and the corporation as a whole. Assistance is provided by planning staffs appropriate to each area of activity. Approvals of long-range plans are principally in the form of authorizations and approvals relating to implementing decisions which are communicated to the responsible organizations.

An aircraft manufacturer reported that the coordination of the long-range plans at the top level of the corporation is accomplished through the executive planning committee. This committee, typically composed of the president, executive vice-president, the vice-presidents of the functional areas, and the director of the long-range planning office, provides a quick reaction group which represents the major areas of the firm and can review, coordinate, and grant formal approval to the plan.

Closely associated with the coordination of long-range planning is the task of reviewing and revalidating existing plans. The review process is an essential keynote to the entire planning activity; from it assumptions, premises, and changed economic conditions for the past period can be used to test the existing applicability of the plan. A review period may be determined by actions of customers or competitors; the development of a new product by a competitor may motivate the review of existing long-term plans in order to develop a competing product. In some cases the marked shift of customers may force a decision on long-term objectives. The companies in the study that are invested heavily in defense production base revisions around the annual Federal Budget determination with adjustment of the company's long-range plans on a six month basis as the customer's budgeting process is completed.

Table 46 reflects the frequency that corporations reporting in the study review their long-range plans. Thirty-six companies report that their plans are reviewed on an annual basis; 30 claim to have their plans under continuous review.[19] One company interviewed reported that

TABLE 46

FREQUENCY CORPORATE LONG-RANGE PLANS ARE REVIEWED

Period	Frequency Reported
Annually	36
Continuously	30
Semi-annually	10
Quarterly	8
Every two years	3

---

[19]This is doubted by the author. What is probably meant is that the groups and individuals responsible for the detailed preparation of the myriad elements of long-range planning continuously review such ancilliary units; it is doubtful if formal review of the master plan is conducted on a continuous basis.

the plans are reviewed on an ad hoc basis when changes in internal or external factors dictate a requirement for review. Another company reports that its review period is based on annual market projections, lead time and effort involved in developing a plan. This same company reports that an attempt is being made to computerize the data for long-range planning so that a continuous review could be made.

It should be recognized that much of the review of the long-range plan is done on a continuous basis as new developments in the planning process are identified. Formal review, however, tends to be effected on specific recurring periods at which time the top management group reviews the overall corporate plans, adjusts corporate goals as required, and directs the establishment of new objectives. This formal review is considered apart from the normal review that the functional area manager conducts relative to his area of responsibility. The period for review varies and depends on the following factors:

1. Functional area involved and the length of time for which the plan has been devised.

2. The dynamics of the competitive environment of the company.

3. The actions of competitors, customers, and government agencies.

4. Internal factors which influence the long-range plan such as mergers, consolidations, or corporate reorganizations.

5. General practices of contemporaries; the general fluctuations of extraordinary actions in the economy which significantly and rapidly obsolete existing long-range plans.

Future Innovations in Long-Range Planning

The existing state of the art in long-range planning is so new both as a concept and a philosophy that one could reasonably expect that many future managerial innovations will be developed and implemented in order to improve and refine present long-range planning. As the long-range planning process is carried out, it is constantly improving and becoming more useful to operating management. As the process is effected, periodical appraisal is conducted, continued efforts are being made to improve existing systems and procedures, and greater sophistication occurs as to methodology in collection and interpretation of planning data. The general improvements contemplated by respondent companies are --

1. Improvements in the collection, evaluation, and dissemination of market intelligence;

2. Improved techniques for advanced identification of product competition which a company elects to enter;

3. Application of computer techniques for such purposes as data retrieving (e.g., market intelligence, technical literature) and simulation exercises designed to optimize product and resource mix;

4. Increased emphasis on personnel development, particularly in long-range planning of personnel requirements and in development of human resources to meet future requirements (notably in management and technical fields);

5. Examination and evaluation of advanced management techniques to achieve improvements in quality, schedule, and cost control;

6. More formalization of the long-range planning effort through spelling out specific responsibility for coordination of the corporate effort;

7. Expansion of staff and increased level of divisional coordination under a single corporate overall plans director, especially in the decentralized, profit center organizational structure;

8. Continued study and selection for use of consultants where such service in no way duplicates the existing in-house capability;

9. Increased emphasis on the use of periodic, well planned seminars;

10. The establishment of charters and regular procedures within the long-range planning framework for evaluating growth contributing projects;

11. Improvement of forecasting procedures; refinement of reflective thinking entered into in the establishment of long-range planning premises and objectives.

A paramount innovation that will lead to improved long-range planning is the integration of long-range planning with higher management development. Anything that is done to help the top management group improve its self-development is itself a long-range plan to provide for the higher organizational requirements of the business. Fenn speaks of the practicality of setting up a local course designed to give the participants an opportunity to examine some of the basic social, political and economic phenomena and to interpret application of these on personal and business lines. Such a course, according to Fenn, gives conferring executives an opportunity to learn how to deal with and reconcile general trends with specific issues that executives face in their day-to-day activities.[20]

---

[20]Dan H. Fenn, *Management In A Rapidly Changing Economy* (New York: McGraw-Hill, 1958), pp. 248-269.

Increasing population growth, complexity of business, and the rapidly advancing technology seem to portend more and more complex planning systems with serious implications for the planning role in corporations in the United States. For large corporations there will probably be a shift from using "administrative assistants" or some such position for long-range planning to a staff agency specifically devoted to long-range planning. There will be less of a tendency than exists in contemporary times to integrate the long and short term planning. However, there will be more attention paid to the relating of long and short-term objective planning. Long-range planning will continue to emerge as a differentiated function of management.

Although the concept of a master plan for all corporate functional areas of effort is relatively new, approximately 57 per cent of the respondent companies indicate the use of a master plan to relate and portray the long-run aspirations of the company. The use of such a plan provides such advantages that the author believes that it will become more useful in the future through providing an integrated decision system for the evaluation of objectives and ancillary plans. In time corporate use of a master plan will become so widespread that businesses will turn increasingly to game theory and other similar methods of optimizing strategy in order to test ancillary plans with master plans.

Not all companies doing long-range planning show a desire to refine existing long-range planning procedures and techniques; 41 per cent indicate that no future refinements are planned. This probably means that they have not identified definite refinements as yet rather than the fact that no future innovations are planned. For some, long-range planning is so new a concept that many of the existing state of the art

procedures have not been mastered, let alone the development of new ones.
Literature on the subject has just emerged; as scholars and practitioners
continue developing new ideas and committing their thinking to writing,
unsophisticated planning systems will be refined.

Chapter Summary

The present chapter has considered the contemporary aspects of
long-range planning in selected American business as reported in the
questionnaire and as gleaned by the author during interviews with corporate planning personnel. The data have been presented in quantitative
fashion wherever possible in order to summarize the information in the
shortest manner possible. Some of the findings did not lend themselves
to quantification, consequently the long-range planning facets were explained in qualitative terms. The author has chosen to forego a formal
summary of the main findings of this chapter in order to integrate such
findings with contemporary literature of the period relating to the major
subjects discussed in this chapter. In the following chapter the main
findings will be integrated with contemporary literature and then reflected as the principal elements in the contemporary philosophy of long-
range planning. Insofar as possible the major and minor subject structure of the next chapter will parallel somewhat that used in the present
chapter; this is believed necessary in order to maintain continuity and
coherence to the presentation. In the main, the following chapter will
be concerned with contemporary literature; however, some impressions
and thoughts of the author concerning long-range planning will also be
included and discussed.

CHAPTER V

CONTEMPORARY PHILOSOPHY OF LONG-RANGE PLANNING IN AMERICAN BUSINESS

Introduction

Preceding decades in American business had fostered the evolution
of planning procedures and techniques to a high degree of refinement as
far as planning for short-range factors in the business was concerned.
The period 1940 through 1950 had seen a realization of the need for the
development of a long-term planning capability in order to meet changing
economic, technological, and political considerations within the economy.
By 1950 the term long-range planning was appearing more and more frequently
in business literature; scholars and practitioners became concerned with
the development of a policy and procedural framework with which to pursue
planning that was projected further into the future than had been experienced by businessmen of the past. It was during the period 1950 through
1961 that the philosophical synthesis of long-range planning was effected.
Management literature of the fifties reflected significant thinking about
long-range planning. This chapter will reflect the long-range planning
thought of the period 1950-1961 as related to the elemental framework
discussed in the previous chapter.

Relationship of Long-Range Planning to
Top Management Hierarchy

Management is the function of executive leadership; planning is
one of the organic functions thereof. The planning function has always
involved a degree of futurity; the higher the organizational level on

which it is performed the more the element of futurity is involved.
Davis in speaking of the responsibilities of top level management in relation to planning notes:

> The social, economic, and business importance of business planning
> tends to increase with the level on which it is performed. Plan-
> ning on the top level of the business organization should be funda-
> mental, far-reaching, and basic.[1]

Although the quality of planning at top levels of an enterprise is of the
greatest importance to the organization, the results of poor planning may
not be apparent until the company has lost an important market, has declined in its financial strength, has become inefficient, or has failed
to accomplish its service objective. By the middle of the 1950's few
chief executives would quarrel with the concept that their principal responsibility was in planning the future of their business. The literature of the contemporary period emphasizes the need for top management
to delegate the operational aspects of the business to subordinates and
concentrate on planning for the future. This did not mean that the chief
executive should concern himself only with long-range planning but that
a considerable portion of his time should be devoted exclusively to a
study of the long-range future and to the timely initiation of plans
and policies necessary to meet anticipated growth and changes in such
things as product, procedures, methods, and organization. In speaking
of the new dimension of long-range planning in the economy and of top
management's responsibility in this respect, Cordiner stated:

> The prime requisite of management is vision. The hallmark of wis-
> dom is the ability to foresee with at least some clarity and confi-

---

[1]Davis, op. cit., p. 51.

dence the needs of tomorrow and beyond tomorrow. If we are to
achieve in fact a glorious economic future, our leaders in business must free themselves of this year's plans and programs and
look at least ten years ahead. The mounting problems and opportunities are making even a decade a short space of time for planning. More and more we should be planning fifteen or twenty years
ahead - an entire business generation.[2]

Long-range corporate planning has always been an activity of top manage-

ment. Before the establishment of a specific organizational entity to

formalize and effect the planning, it was performed by the board chair-

man and the president. A fundamental difference here was that the plan-

ning was effected by a few key individuals at the top of the hierarchy

and was done on an informal basis which did not entail the formality

with which contemporary executive personnel approach the task of long-

range planning.

An intimate relationship exists between top management and long-

range planning. Not only does top management devote most of its time to

long-range planning but it must continually be cognizant of the necessity

for compatibility between long and short-range planning. No other group

in the corporate structure is better equipped to define the desired role

of the company in its future environment. The acceptance by top manage-

ment personnel of their responsibilities in planning for the future of

the business stimulated the growing interest in long-range planning.

Long-range planning began to evolve as a formal technique necessary in

order to assure survival in the competitive environment. By the late

1950's management literature had reached a relatively high degree of re-

[2]Ralph J. Cordiner, Speech to the Economic Club of New York, as
reported in The Harbus News, December 21, 1956.

finement; managers and scholars began to evaluate and improve management techniques and practices which had been neglected because of the demands of World War II and the post-war period. Long-term planning was one area which received attention during this period.

The Definition of Long-Range Planning

As yet no standard and comprehensive definition of long-range planning has been formulated; however, it is believed that such a definition should include the following elements:

1. Long-range planning is an orderly analysis of external economic factors affecting the company as a whole.

2. Long-range planning contemplates all internal factors, forces, and effects of the organization.

3. Long-range planning contains a high degree of futurity.

4. As performed by the top-management group, it has to do with broad over-all programs and policies important to the organization as a whole.

5. Long-range planning, as an executive process, encompasses all functional areas of the organization; all aspects of the organization which may change in the future are evaluated in the process.

6. In the truest sense, long-range planning is a formalized process accomplished throughout the organizational structure; a specific staff agency exists as a focal point for the process.

7. Long-range planning is carried on by the institutional mind of the organization and as such exists as a concept beyond the frame of reference of a single individual.

8. It coordinates all the people and functions of a company and involves much more than business forecasting.

9. As an intellectual process, long-range planning prepares the corporate entity to adjust to future conditions; in its conceptual sense long-range planning shapes the future according to a corporate image.

10. Long-range planning is effected within a moral, social, and ethical framework; it facilitates accomplishing the service objective of the organization.

11. It is not forecasting; long-range planning is necessary precisely because one cannot forecast. It does not deal with future decisions; it deals with the futurity of present decisions. It does not attempt to eliminate risk; rather it identifies the proper risks that must be assumed by the business.[3]

12. Long-range planning is not an entity in itself; its primary purpose is to provide the guidelines necessary for vital decision making throughout the organization.

An inclusion of the preceding elements into a definition of long-range planning would create a definition so long and unwieldly that it would serve no practical purpose. Consequently, the author elects to shorten the definition, but at the same time express the necessity of contemplating the elemental framework of long-range planning as indicated in any use of the term. Long-range planning is that activity whereby a systematic effort to collect and analyze significant economic, technological, political, social, and market data needed as a basis for forecasting events and conditions one or more years in the future is effected. This planning then outlines how the company will acquire and use resources to achieve its business goals and objectives in the forecast period.

---

[3]Drucker, op. cit., pp. 238-240.

The Purpose of Long-Range Planning

In evaluating the purpose of long-range planning one must realize that accurate planning beyond one year is difficult at best, and that long-range plans are very apt to be changed before completion; nevertheless such planning serves a definite purpose in setting up an orderly approach to the problems of long-range growth of the company. Long-range planning is an important factor in the continued development of product, plant, organization, and company policy. Any long-term planning effort has as one of its important purposes the continuous study and interpretation of industry influences on the business as a whole. The adequacy of the product line is continuously re-examined in the light of the industry trends to be sure that an expansion of the marketing capability of the organization is effected in order to perform its service objective. Another purpose is to provide for the conduct of operations over the long term so as to supply an adequate cushion for short-term reverses. Such implies a requirement for defensive as well as offensive plans and programs. Political forces may effect a complete reversal of economic trends which can be catastrophic to the company without any long-term plans upon which it can base its decisions. Long-range planning forces management thinking and planning under conditions designed to protect company growth and stability under different sets of possible circumstances.

Long-range planning is not an entity in itself. Its primary purpose is to provide the guidelines necessary for the decision-making processes throughout the organization. It is adopted to obtaining, translating, understanding, and disseminating of information which will help to improve the rationality of current decisions which are based upon future expectations. These expectations are developed through a process of forecasting and contemplating the future. Long-range planning has as another purpose the minimization of the proper risks in the future and the insuring of optimum results from the employment of the factors of production. While it does not eliminate risk, it does point out the <u>right</u> risk which the business should assume in its future operations. Long-range planning enables management to avoid the pitfalls of short-range decisions which do not contemplate the long-range objectives of the business. It enables corporate management to develop and build the organization according to a predetermined corporate image.

Determining How Far Ahead To Plan

Most literature cites three to five years as the most common long-range planning term. The length of time for which plans are made varies widely from company to company. In some instances long-range plans are confined to one year ahead while in others they are measured in terms of decades. Even in individual companies the period varies widely depending upon the subject or functional area of effort under consideration. Drucker, in writing of the time periods of planning, says, ". . . the essence of planning is to make present decisions with knowledge of their futurity. It is the futurity that determines the time span, and not vice versa."[4] According to Drucker it is the type of business and the nature of the decision which determine the time spans of planning. The time decision is the first and a highly important risk-taking decision in the planning process, with the time decision as a result of the character and nature of the business.

-----

[4]Drucker, <u>op</u>. <u>cit</u>., p. 244.

There should be some logic in selecting the right time range for a company's planning; in all probability a company should not plan for a period longer than is economically justifiable. Koontz and O'Donnell have developed the "commitment principle" or the concept that planning should encompass the period of time necessary to fulfill the commitments involved.[5] This implies that there is no uniform or arbitrary length of time for which a given company should plan but rather the period is based on various plans depending on the commitment involved.

The National Industrial Conference Board, reporting on a survey of business planning in 1952 disclosed that businesses varied considerably in the period for which they planned. But three to five years appeared to be the most common term for long-range planning, and few companies planned less than a year in advance.[6]

Observation of business planning leads to the belief that the long-run period tends to be selected on the basis of a period of years in which management feels that predictions bear an acceptable degree of validity.[7] While there appears to be a somewhat arbitrary selection of planning periods by businessmen, there is some uniformity between the planning periods of the major functional areas of effort.

---

[5]Harold Koontz and Cyril O'Donnell, Principles of Management (New York: McGraw-Hill Book Company, Inc., 1959), pp. 467-468.

[6]"Industry Plans For The Future," Conference Board Business Record, vol. 9, pp. 324-328 (August, 1952).

[7]Koontz and O'Donnell, op. cit., p. 467.

It is believed that the overall corporate long-range planning period should be considered as that time dimension in which the necessary functional and additional areas of effort are planned so as to provide for an orderly and efficient employment of the factors of production in the accomplishment of the organizational service objective with relation to a specific corporate goal. This provides an appreciation and consideration of the many factors, forces, and effects which influence the corporate planning period. Thus if a corporation is planning capital expenditures ten years ahead and executive development only five years ahead there may be a dis-equilibrium of planning which could have an adverse effect on attainment of the corporate objective. It is believed that there should be a harmony of the future period for which long-term plans are made; as a rule the planning period seems to be based on an economic projection which follows normal trends without regard to cyclical fluctuations in the economy. A company should plan as far ahead as is useful but only so far as it is possible to do so with reasonable accuracy.

Organization for Long-Range Planning

Any review of the organizational structure that is used by business and industrial concerns for accomplishing long-range planning should be prefaced with an examination of the theory and concept of organization as contemplated by some of the industrial and academic authorities in the field of management. In accomplishing this review care should be taken to identify some of the major criteria that such authorities establish in order to determine the best organizational structure for long-term planning. Long-term plans, as the product of the planning processes, should emerge from such executive participation as to insure their installation if and when they are ratified by the Board of Directors. The method of determining how plans are formulated is inherently related to how the formal organization is structured for accomplishing the planning. Many alternatives exist and a variety of organizational structures are in use in management practice today. Some appear to be more efficient and more in line with advanced philosophies of management.

Line and Staff in Long-Range Planning

It was noted previously that plans should emerge from participation to assure their installation when ratified. Basically two fundamental types of organizational elements can be used to create long-term plans, via., the line or the staff. A third method of organization is added by taking a combination of the two basic organizational concepts to form an interdependent line-staff structure to effect long-range planning. The line hierarchy of functions extends downward throughout the organization and makes possible a division of labor and primary specialization in the creation or distribution of certain salable values. This is the primary chain of command, i.e., the scale of responsibility and authority that is correlated directly with the hierarchy of the line function.[8] The staff agency, on the other hand, in any organized activity is set up for the purpose of providing the chief executive and the heads of the operating departments with certain specialized assistance. In addition the staff agency relieves the chief executive of part of his burden by analyzing and studying operations and problems in order to provide information

---

[8] R. C. Davis, "What The Staff Function Actually Is," _Advanced Management_ (May, 1954), p. 14.

which will enable the line executive to reach sound conclusions in his work. Basically the staff officer, whether in the military establishment or in business, is an advisor, an extension of the personality and authority of the line official whom he serves. If a staff agency makes the long-range plans, operating in a vacuum with no representation or established contact with line operations there is a high degree of risk that although the plans will be accepted by higher authorities in line capacities there will be little enthusiasm for the wholehearted implementation of the plans. And it is the line official who can give energetically to the success or failure of the plan when it is put into operation.

Obtaining Participation in Long-Range Planning

Participation in all planning affects a manager's area of authority (through his being informed, contributing suggestions, and evaluating alternative courses of action) and contributes to good planning, loyalty and overall managerial effectiveness. Although it is difficult in large companies to have a great deal of direct participation, methods exist by which the same end can be accomplished. One is the use of a long-range planning staff to provide assistance and counsel to the line official. Another technique often suggested is a planning committee; such committees established at appropriate levels throughout the organization can be effective in transmitting planning information, eliciting suggestions, serving as media for the release of the ideas of the line officials, and giving them a feeling of having contributed to the development of the plan. In speaking of the value of participation Davis says:

> The greatest practicable participation in the performance of any managerial functions is desirable, provided that there are no important violations of the principles of unity of command, direction, or single accountability. Participation promotes an under-

standing of the activity. It develops an interest in it and improves morale. It makes maximum use of the brains and ability of
the organization. The Principle of Participation says: A feeling
of "worth-whileness" and "belonging" tends to develop from participation in the making of decisions underlying the accomplishment of organizational objectives. It tends to integrate the interests and abilities of individuals with the organization's purpose.[9]

The idea of participation has some special significance in terms of the

development of a long-range planning philosophy. Most contemporary lit-

erature still indicates that basic decisions are made by "top manage-

ment" and that top management delegates certain basic decisions. But,

according to Drucker this reflects yesterday's rather than today's

reality. While he recognizes that top management has the final respon-

sibility, the business enterprise of today is no longer an organization

in which there are a handful of managers at the top who make the deci-

sions and a group of workers at the bottom who carry out the orders.

The organization is, according to Drucker,

. . . Primarily an organization of professionals of highly specialized, knowledge exercising autonomous, responsible judgment. And
every one of them--whether manager or individual expert contribu-
tor--constantly makes truly entrepreneurial decisions, that is,
decisions which affect the economic characteristics and risks of
the entire enterprise. He makes them not by 'delegation from above'
but inevitably in the performance of his own job and work.[10]

Under this concept the idea of participation in the formulation of

long-range plans takes on special significance: the manager must know

what direction the organization is headed and what goals are established

if he is to participate in both the daily operational matters and in

the reflective thinking necessary to develop the long-range plans.

---

[9]Ralph Currier Davis, The Fundamentals of Top Management (New York:
Harper & Brothers, Publishers, 1951), p. 200.

[10]Drucker, op. cit., p. 242.

A conflict in management philosophies exists with regard to the need for greater participation in the planning processes. Long-range plans are often so confidential and important that it is risky to bring into the final decision or commitment making process those executive individuals who might resign and join competition. How can these two considerations be reconciled? In this regard Steiner has said:

> There are devices by which some companies seek to resolve the problem of personal participation in planning. Among these are planning staffs, so-called "bottom-up" planning, "grass roots" budgeting, management clubs, and a general effort through various organizational and personnel policies to instill a sense of participation in plans involving the destinies of the enterprise. All these have been effective, but I feel much fruitful work can be done in developing new techniques, refining old techniques, and getting deeper knowledge of what part individuals should play as individuals in improved planning.[11]

The corporate management is caught on the horns of a dilemma for it is conceded that the complete separation of planning from operations might be in error. Although a company may establish a staff agency composed of trusted individuals, the possibility still exists that this staff, through close and frequent contact with line officials could result in a possible compromise to the company's confidential long-range plans. Nevertheless the long-range planning must be rooted in what has been and what is. It requires the participation of operating executives, for much of it must be based on their experience and they must participate if they are to accept the plans wholeheartedly.

An indication of the degree to which corporate managers consider their long-range plans as classified information is afforded in the

---

[11] Steiner, op. cit., p. 97.

study under discussion. All but one of the participating companies specifically requested that their names not be used in the study in conjunction with their specific methodology in long-range planning. Although the author requested that the cooperating companies provide company regulations, standard operating procedures, literature, organizational charts, policy instruments, and such related publications as the company used directly in its long-range planning activities, only two companies out of the 79 responding favorably to the study provided the information requested. Over half of the respondents indicated that such media was "confidential," "restricted," or "for company use only." The companies interviewed were reluctant to discuss their long-range plans, although they did cooperate in providing general information as to their philosophy and methodology.

Alternative Organization for Long-Range Planning

Newman believes that long-range planning units should normally report to the senior executive, inasmuch as they perform a function which he would perform if he had the time and specialized ability. If this puts too many division executives under the immediate supervision of seniors, Newman thinks the solution may lie in a setup comparable to the Chief of Staff in the Army who supervises all staff divisions and otherwise acts as the senior executive's alter ego. Of course this system would have the disadvantage of subordinating the staff units; on the organization chart the long-range planners would be a couple of boxes away from the senior executive. However, they would be partially compensated by the status and prestige of the "chief of staff" who would definitely be in the top hierarchy.[12]

---

[12]William H. Newman, Administrative Action (New York, Prentice-Hall, Inc., 1951), pp. 324-328.

In addition to utilizing existing company talent for the development of long-term plans the services of an outside economist or management consultant can be used. This approach should not be used, however, except possibly in the development of specialized areas of the plans which are beyond the scope of the corporation personnel capabilities or for information which is used so infrequently that it would not pay to have a full time economic staff to provide the data. Two serious drawbacks to dependence on outside professional services seem to exist, viz., first, when a consultant does the work he and not the company gets the experience of studying out and thinking out the real problem. Second, the personnel in the company doing a particular kind of work have a real background of the company, its problems and its approach to doing business that cannot be expected of an outsider, however capable. Wrapp, in speaking of the use of management or economic consultants for the long-range planning process states that the understanding and confidence in a plan can only come from months of painstaking development by the managers concerned who will be responsible for carrying out the plans during the implementation stage. According to Wrapp:

> I do not deny that at certain stages a special staff or a management consultant may be indispensable to a company planning group. Rather, someone with technical knowledge or broad experience in a market or industry quite often can assist tremendously by bringing a fresh and objective point of view to bear. But specialists lose their advantage when complete responsibility for the planning is turned over to them, and, unfortunately, many companies have foundered on this "easy" course of action. Part of the gain to be secured in long-range planning is the thinking-through that the company itself must do, without regard for whether it ends up as pieces of paper with words and graphs on them.[13]

---

[13]H. Edward Wrapp, "Organization For Long-Range Planning," Harvard Business Review (January-February, 1957), p. 44.

There appears to be no short-cut or easy solution to planning for the future of a company; it is hard work; it cannot be done by a separate group of people isolated from the other operations of the company. A plan formulated entirely by others and presented to management as a completed document indicates that management is abrogating certain of its organic functions. And in the final analysis management is the only group which today has and tomorrow should have the responsibility for the well-being of the company. A concept of long-range planning as envisioned in this paper means that the program cannot be the product of one man or a small group of men; no one individual or small group of individuals has the breadth of knowledge of the many functional areas of business required to develop a plan in which management will have any confidence. The work should be directed by someone who is in more or less continuous contact with the different managers concerned so that the results represent a team approach and an integration of the functional and additional areas of consideration of the corporate entity as a whole, not as segmented parts.

The utilization of a centralized staff agency or group to coordinate the planning activities of the decentralized units has considerable merit. This does not mean that planning committees should be eliminated or that the benefits of having the key members of the organization participate in the preparation of the plans will be negated. It merely means that the operating officials should be relieved of as many of the details, technical calculations, and data gathering as possible. One of the primary considerations in designing the top management structure is to provide for strategic planning which involves seeing that activities like research and development, market research, organization planning, facilities planning, and other aspects of long-range planning are provided where applicable. It also includes building coordinated strategic planning into top management processes.

Another danger exists in organizing for long-range planning primarily around a specialized staff. Although a specialized staff is set up to aid in the planning function the contingency exists that the staff may assume that its role is planning rather than in facilitating the planning activities of the line managers. Left to its own discretion the staff may proceed to set up objectives, goals, and plans according to its own conceptions and premises. Such staffs may have a further tendency to equate their forecasting of the future environment with planning and to assume that their company will automatically adopt its operations to their predictions. It should be remembered that the responsibility for the planning function cannot be delegated; it is a basic part of the manager's job. Yeoman service can be obtained from the planning staff if it is relegated to its proper position as providing technical services, advice, and counsel to the line officials.

Management literature reflects a growing realization that good long-range planning must proceed both up and down the organizational structure. It begins at the top with the setting of objectives and the tentative formulation of broad programs and policies for accomplishing the corporate objectives. After the basics of the long-range planning has been established, the operating divisions and the staff agencies can be brought into active involvement in planning. The pay-off of bringing in the collective knowledge of the entire organization is reflected

in three dividends. According to Cassels and Randall,

> First, it greatly reduces the likelihood that you will be led
> astray by a false assumption or a front-office misunderstanding
> of the actual problems on the firing line. Second, it helps to
> stimulate creative thinking deep within the organization, be-
> cause it provides a specific channel by which such thinking can
> be expressed. Third, it gives the men who must carry out a plan
> a sense of personal identification with it—a feeling that they
> were in on the take-off. This leads to more enthusiastic and
> imaginative execution.[14]

There are no stereotyped rules to follow in the organization of

the planning group since each company must use the individual advantages

inherent in its own organization. Fisch and Jacoby, in indicating two

specific areas which are crucial to the successful accomplishment of

long-range planning, note:

1. The planning group should be drawn from within the company

organization. The use of consultants is best confined to a staff or ad-

visory position, and to specific studies and information-gathering pro-

jects, particularly in the initial or experimental stages of long-range

planning. The final plan itself will be more readily accepted if it is

assembled by company personnel.

2. Members of the group should be of diversified background and

interest and no one department should be allowed to dominate the in-

vestigation and formation of the plan. This is an important aspect of

insuring objectivity. Practice varies from company to company concern-

ing the final choice of personnel for the planning group. The chairman

should be a ranking member of top management, both as an indication of

---

[14]Louis Cassels and Raymond L. Randall, "Long-Range Planning,"
Nation's Business (August, 1961) p. 83.

the importance of the plan to management and of top level support for the planning process. On the other hand, key junior executives who are unusually objective and incisive in their thinking can also play a vital role in the planning group. It goes almost without saying that the group should be authorized to draw upon any department or group within the company as specialized skills or knowledge are required.[15]

Summary of Organization for Long-Range Planning

In the past few years many companies have established full time positions and offices to effect long-range planning. The establishment of these positions represents the creation of a new role in the hierarchy of many U.S. corporations. In the past American businesses through line executives have done long-range planning to one degree or another, usually each doing the long-range planning with the aid of some staff specialists in his own area of endeavor—manufacturing, engineering, marketing, personnel, or manpower. There has also been some evidence that a generalist type planner with a title such as "assistant to the president," "executive vice president," or "executive vice president, administration," has existed to perform a general type of coordination of long-range planning throughout the entire corporate system. The current trend toward decentralization has accelerated the need for a more formal organizational structure for long-range planning as well as a new kind of planning at company headquarters, which is more abstract but which nevertheless sets goals and allocates resources among the various "self-contained" planning

---

[15]Gerald F. Fisch and Dean L. Jacoby, "Long-Range Planning—An Approach to Leadership," Cost and Management (April, 1959), p. 147.

systems. By the late 1950's large American businesses were formally organizing long-range planning offices in consonance with the developing philosophy of long-range planning.

The Accomplishment of Long-Range Planning

The Establishment of Objectives for Long-Range Planning

The problem of setting necessary objectives for long-range planning is a fundamental task for management. Objectives that are established should be realistic, attainable and compatible with the organizational service objective. The first basic question to be resolved in setting long-range planning objectives is what kind of business the company desires to be in when the time period for which objectives have been established arrives. Only top management can decide after some preliminary reflective thinking and long-range planning is accomplished. Basic analysis is called for and includes, but is not necessarily limited to, an examination of the key influences in the growth of the industry and the strategic and tactical position of the company as compared to its present and potential competitors. One of the decisive factors to consider is the desired rate of expansion; limiting factors are both external and internal. The internal factors include all of the functional and other areas where long-range planning is required but is most important in the areas of production, distribution, and finance. The citation of the previous three areas is not meant to distract from the importance of the others; no one factor is the "key" to expansion. Rather, expansion should be considered as an objective which requires the harmonious balance of all functions, factors, forces and effects in order to accomplish the long-range goal.

Another basic question which businessmen consider in long-range planning is whether objectives should be projected on a trend or a cyclical basis. In the latter case management tries to plan its moves in light of forecasts of cyclical fluctuations; in the former it does not. Cresap supports the "trend" basis:

> The long-term development of a business should be geared to long-term movements and should not be governed by guesses as to short-term swings. Employment of the latter procedure involves a company in the risk of being strategically whip-sawed and of losing its position in growing markets. The 'trend' approach to planning accepts the fact that there will be periods (of a reasonably short duration, it is hoped) when some plant capacity will be temporarily idle. But such an approach recognizes that, if the alternative is to delay action in the face of reliable indicators of future market growth--to delay for 'more favorable circumstances' --action should be taken.
>
> In fact, it is more speculative to attempt to time long-term strategical development by cyclical guesswork as to the 'right moment' than to move ahead sure-footedly when the distant signal is clearly "green" at the same time assessing the extent of the risks involved and reflecting this assessment in the long-term plan by appropriate provisions for periods of retrenchment. Reasonable periods of idle plant capacity are far less costly than the loss of basic competitive and market status.[16]

There is some evidence that intermediate planning should take into account cyclical position. Long-range planning should not; it should be based on secular trend. The objective setting should be limited to major areas of consideration and should start with a careful study of the industry environment as a basis for appraising the company's position and its strenths and limitations.

The process of long-range planning should begin with the establishment of basic objectives; policies which direct effort to the objectives then require formulation upon this basis when a course of action

---

[16] Mark W. Cresap, Jr., "Some Guides to Long-Term Planning," N.A.C.A. Bulletin (January, 1958), p. 602.

is prepared. The long-range plan then consists of the objectives, policies, and the subsiciary plans necessary to accomplish the long-term objectives. However, for a company to reach its goals established in the basic plans or programs of action usually encompass a more limited time period. What then, is the relationship between objectives and subsidiary plans? According to Steiner:

> Objectives are reasonably stable but subsidiary plans and programs can be modified more readily as events dictate. The objectives and policies set the tone, direction, timing, environment, and patterns for evolving decisions to achieve selected objectives. Concrete short-range decisions when strung end to end should, over time, result in the achievement of the goals of a plan. As time moves forward, short-range events can, of course, indicate a need for altering longer-range policies and goals. Long-range planning is therefore a continuous process.[17]

Objectives, however specific must be related to a time table in the planning process. Answering the key question "when" is necessary before any real planning can be accomplished and the dovetailing of collateral and subordinate plans can be effected. The heart of strategic business planning is defining objectives; but accomplishment of these objectives must be done within the time dimensions of the internal and economic external factors affecting the firm.

Pretesting of Long-Range Planning

It was reported in Chapter IV that contemporary literature is almost devoid of writings on the subject of the pretesting of long-range plans. Techniques used by industry vary in intensity and type; management judgment appears to be the principal method. Contemporary litera-

---

[17]George A. Steiner, "What Do We Know About Using Long-Range Plans?" California Management Review (Fall, 1959), p. 93.

ture, however, has made a few suggestions regarding the testing of long-range plans. One way of testing long-range plans has been suggested which entails trying out the plan in a tightly controlled "pilot plant" operation before committing the company to the full program. For the pilot run there must be cross checks and duplicate sources of information to insure the accuracy of the plan. All possible alternatives must be considered and tested. Outside groups should be freely used to test and corroborate the work of internal groups.[18] The difficulty of this approach stems mainly from the problem of applying such a technique to a company which has a comprehensive and integrated long-term plan where creating the future environmental conditions is almost impossible. While such a testing technique may be used for a specific plan, as a product plan, it is believed unwieldly and expensive for a plan of any magnitude.

The testing of long-range plans must be considered from two fundamental points, viz., the tools to be used and the process to go through to accomplish the evaluation. The existence of a formal long-range planning function does not necessarily guarantee good plans; nor does the availability of many "testing tools" insure that the proper evaluation of the plan can be effected. The value of the planning activity can be elusive since a period of years must elapse before a set of long-range plans can be evaluated on the basis of results and performance. Consequently, there is the very real possibility that the long-range planning activity can produce ineffective or unprofitable plans which

---

[18]Gerald G. Fisch and Dean L. Jacoby, "Long-Range Planning--An Approach to Leadership," Cost and Management (April, 1959), p. 147.

go undetected for months or years. To prevent the creation of misleading plans management is desirous of subjecting the planning activity to whatever objective tests can be developed. As Platt and Maines envision:

Pretests of plans not only reveal flaws but encourage bolder approaches to future planning. If a company has no experimental means by which to make its planning mistakes inexpensively, it tends to adopt plans that have proved themselves in the past-- and avoid those which, although promising, do depart sufficiently from experience to pose severe risks. Conservative behavior is a natural consequence of the lack of valid experimental techniques.[19]

If management can pretest its plans in a "decision laboratory," the cost of full scale or actual tests can be eliminated and possibly better plans devised. Pretesting, says Platt, may be somewhat new to businessmen but certainly not so to the scientist. "In business and industry, on the other hand, until now there has been no corresponding laboratory. The world of experience has been the only way to test policies, decisions, and planning."[20] The lack of literature on the subject of the testing of long-range plans leads one to believe that much remains to be innovated in this important area of long-range planning. As was noted in the previous chapter many of the companies indicated that future refinements in the corporate planning process would be directed to developing methodology for the testing of plans. In all probability this will come about as businesses become more proficient in long-range planning.

_____

[19] William J. Platt and N. Robert Maines, "Pretest Your Long-Range Plan," Harvard Business Review (January-February, 1959), p. 119.

[20] Ibid., p. 120.

Difficulties and Limitations of Long-Range Planning

Contemporary literature reflects some of the difficulties and
problems encountered in the long-range planning process. Neuhoff and
Thompson, in a survey of company planning practices, reported that most
difficulties stemmed from governmental controls or industry peculiarities.
Comments on these difficulties follow:

> Government Controls - Unfortunately, our company has been unable
> to put into effect very many of those things which have been
> planned, because we do not wish to indulge in long-term financ-
> ing for the purpose, and the government's unrealistic and unsound
> taxing policy on corporations has been such that after taxes we
> have found ourselves unable, in many instances, to make the nec-
> essary improvements. The result of this has been that our plant
> has suffered seriously in the last few years. --Foundries

> Because government policies and controls affect our business to a
> very great extent, all of our planning is, as far as possible, sub-
> ject to revision, in case government policies that affect the con-
> struction industry change. This is, of course, no happy situation
> for us, because there is always a great element of uncertainty.
> --Building Materials

> Industry Peculiarities - We do not plan for longer than one year.
> The machine tool business is of such a cyclical nature that our
> plans are continually being altered to suit the variations that
> occur. --Machine Tools

> The trouble with future planning in a highly cyclical industry is
> that, while it has great utility, it is hard to combat the psy-
> chological factors involved. When business is good, there is a
> tendency to expand and provide for large expenditures. As soon
> as business slumps, everybody wants to contract. There is a ten-
> dency to base decisions on present-day conditions rather than on
> the planning program. --Machinery[21]

Other difficulties are evident because in many companies the feeling still persists that planning is the main function of the chairman and
the president; vice presidents and lower echelons should concentrate on
running the company. Then too, budgets, performance ratings, and bonuses

---

[21]Malcolm C. Neuhoff and G. Clark Thompson, "Industry Plans For
The Future," Business Record (August, 1952), p. 326.

almost always are focused on the near term; accomplishment toward the
long-range goals are most difficult to measure. Many executives regard
the development of a long-range plan as a meddlesome nuisance which dis-
tracts from the orderly accomplishment of daily activities. In many instances it is the subtle resistance that destroys the long-range planning
effort. In this respect Wrapp says:

> Indeed, I would venture the hypothesis that the most serious ob-
> stacle to long-range planning is not so much the drain on manage-
> ment time, the actual problems of doing good planning, or the dan-
> ger of revealing company strategy, as it is the subtle, but oc-
> casionally open, opposition of some executives which appears in
> the early stages of the development.[22]

Another limitation or rather danger of long-range planning is recognized by Shelley and Pearson. According to them, over-sophistication
of the long-range planning activity may be harmful to the company that
is not equipped to study the social, economic, political and technological factors of long-range planning. As Shelley and Pearson say:

> High quality long-range planning is not the same in every company.
> One would expect much greater sophistication from a company like
> Du Pont or General Electric than from a company that doesn't even
> make formal annual plans. To avoid offering a stock approach, we
> purposely did not include a format for long-range planning. Some
> companies are perfectly capable of dealing in economic indexes
> like GNP, population trends, and the like. Others would merely
> be confused and discouraged by the mention of cyclical, economic,
> and technological trends. But both types of companies can and do
> make effective long-range plans.[23]

Other difficulties and dangers of long-range planning exist. One
is to assume that planning decisions will be carried out without machinery for implementation; another is inflexibility in planning at one ex-

---

[22]Wrapp, op. cit., p. 39.

[23]Tulley Shelley, Jr., and Andrall W. Pearson, "A Blue-Print For
Long-Range Planning," Business Horizons (July, 1961), p. 84.

treme and abandoning the plan under pressure at the other extreme. Prudent management may very well review the timing of plans in periods of stress but should avoid abandoning the long-range plan unless clearly indicated. Another difficulty is that of confusing background studies and forecasting with planning; a long-range plan has specific objectives and establishes definite paths to follow in achieving the objectives. Forecasting is complementary to long-range planning and is a projection of what is expected to happen in the future. As envisioned by Steiner,

> A plan takes a forecast as given, together with many other considerations, and determines feasible goals and means to reach them. As events differ from forecasts, planning steps are altered, but not necessarily the broad objectives. Good planning requires continuous checking on events and forecasts and consequent modification of plans and courses of action toward goals. Similarly, background studies of particular subjects -- consumer habits, capital markets, or marketing a product, for example -- are not plans unless they contain the attributes of plans and are executed as plans.[24]

Many other reasons exist to cause plans to fall. Lack of support from top management, undue separation of planning from operations, failure to put plans in writing, and failure to make timely decisions, are but a few which may be cited. Notwithstanding the existence of such possible contingencies, there is evidence that some large American businesses participate actively in long-range planning, thus indicating that most of the difficulties and limitations involved in long-range planning have been largely overcome.

---

[24]George A. Steiner, "What Do We Know About Using Long-Range Plans," California Management Review (Fall, 1959), p. 102.

Extra-Organizational Factors Affecting Long-Range Planning

External factors play an important part in the development of meaningful plans for a company's future. Any firm which establishes long-range plans, whether they be expressed in terms of volume, of capital outlay programs, of profits, of service, or of new products, is likely to find many variables which should be reviewed for their economic validity. Business is affected intimately by a great many factors beyond its control such as the general level of prosperity in the country, access to foreign markets, tariff protection against imports, foreign exchange rate trends, general availability of money for capital, government controls, and a host of other economic factors which must be identified and evaluated as part of the long-range planning process. Other factors such as the effect of trends in the Gross National Product Components, taxation and fiscal policy, foreign trade movements, and political movements such as the European Common Market all have an influence on the general economic climate and as such are considerations that must be evaluated. Long-range planning deals mainly with the projection of certain basic trends, viz.,

General economic conditions
Population growth
Population shifts as between age groups
Changes in consumer spending patterns
Substitutions, new competitive products, and technological changes
Changes in the percent of the market
Industrial production shifts

For a particular company the general economic factors of the economy are a consideration; from this point the general parameters that gauge the growth of the company as a whole are of fundamental importance. As the development of the plan proceeds, the economic factors gradually shift to those factors over which the business has some control.

Koontz and O'Donnell have called certain economic factors planning premises that are non-controllable in the sense that the individual firm doing the planning cannot do anything about them. These premises include such things as population growth, future price levels, political environment, tax rates and policies, and business cycles.[25] Trends in the national economy and in a particular industry often may have more bearing on company profits than the efforts within a company. Consequently the plans should isolate these external trends and draw conclusions as to their influence on the particular company and its products. Although the company cannot change these economic factors and trends it can develop its plan so as to take the maximum advantage of competitive position.

Economic factors are not just related to the general economy and the individual company's position in the market. The evaluation should also include a careful appraisal of what competitors are doing with their product lines, prices, distribution methods, and their long-range planning. This provides for the development of alternative plans which are in a strategic position with relation to other companies in the industry; it keeps the initiative away from competition and keeps them on the defensive.

An evaluation of extra-organizational factors relative to long-range planning is accomplished through the interpretation of available statistics and other pertinent information on the economy. Planning involves the making of assumptions and decisions about the future growth based on the input of statistical and other data. Although there is an

---

[25]Koontz and O'Donnell, op. cit., p. 478.

element of risk involved, two fundamental things can be accomplished to minimize these risks:

1. Temper the corporate long-term planning to the basic trends in the economy rather than to forecasts of yearly fluctuations in the business cycle.

2. Plan for fluctuations in the economy and long-term changes in the political, technological, social, and legislative climate.

Forecasting in Long-Range Planning

Much has been written in contemporary literature concerning forecasting; relatively little of this has been directed to the relationship between long-range planning and forecasting. Chapter IV reflected that long-range planning was necessary precisely because business cannot forecast accurately. Forecasting was envisioned as an attempt to predict the most probable course of events; long-range planning adjusts long-range plans to take advantage of the forecast events. Planning is the activity occurring after forecasting and is designed to prepare the organization for acceptance of the proper risks in the future.

Much of the forecasting can be delegated to staff groups but the planning from these forecasts remains as a distinct line responsibility. General economic forecasting is a distinct responsibility and is used as a preliminary first step in the forecasting of sales and other corporate activities; practically all of the companies studied reported a program for forecasting.

It should be understood that forecasting is the projection of future business conditions and company performance as related to the environment. Forecasting per se does not include the function of altering company policies to take advantage of or protect against projected business conditions although important management decisions may very well result from the forecast. Forecasting is lacking in the innate function of _acting_ to effect the course of company progress. As to the differentiation of long-range planning from forecasting, LeBreton and Henning say:

> Planning's distinction from forecasting is complicated by the fact that forecasting is used in planning in two ways. First, the planner attempts to predict what actions other people will take, what future conditions will exist, and then builds his future course of action based on these predictions. Second, he tries to predict what the results of his plans will be -- or rather he determines what conditions he would like to bring about and then establishes his plan to accomplish this. Thus we find forecasting, like decision-making, an integral part of the planning process, but at the same time something different and distinguishable from planning itself.[26]

It is entirely possible for a forecast to indicate action that is contradictory to that indicated by existing long-range plans; in fact one of the methods of testing the validity of the long-term plan is to apply the current forecasts to it for compatibility.

Forecasting, as a somewhat formal function is generally practiced as the function of a relatively small group of people within a department isolated from the mainstream of company long-range planning. The function of the group is clear cut: given the present competitive position of the firm, what will the effect of future economic, legislative, technological, and other factors of the environment be on the long-term objectives of the firm. Forecasts as developed are based on both internal and external data; the latter are more involved and less predictable.

---

[26]Preston P. LeBreton and Dale A. Henning, _Planning Theory_ (Englewood Cliffs, New Jersey, Prentice-Hall, Inc., 1961), p. 8.

The point should be underscored that all businessmen forecast in one way or another; they cannot escape forecasting while they remain responsible for the business enterprise. The businessman can forecast by hunch, by intuition, by judgment, or he can bring the forecasting activities of his enterprise within the more definite and tangible boundaries of an organized management function on a somewhat formal basis. Unorganized business forecasting is perhaps the product of personal judgment, intuition, and sometimes perhaps only a subconscious feeling of the course of future events. It is more an art than a science on this basis and it will remain in this somewhat unsatisfactory state until its methods can be brought into the realm of the rational and can be based on logical relationships that govern business behavior and can be stated in measurable terms. According to Newbury,

> There can be no intelligent or effective planning for a business enterprise without the preliminary step of forecasting. The planned objectives of management can be realized only when there is a reasonably accurate forecast of the trend of general business and of the sales income of the specific company. The businessman cannot act on the spur of the moment. Successful management requires that the businessman look ahead and make plans. In short, he must plan, and he must forecast in order that he can plan.[27]

The Benefits of Long-Range Planning

Long-range planning has been described by some management authorities as profit insurance. It considers profit not only in terms of the actual dollars but also as a percentage return on investment. The magazine Nation's Business for November, 1957, reported a study of 400 com-

---

[27]Frank D. Newbury, Business Forecasting; Principles and Practice (New York: McGraw-Hill, 1952), p. 4.

panies covering an eighteen-year period. The study revealed that a large percentage of successful and profitable corporations used long-range planning; that a low percentage of the less profitable ones did so. The foregoing is one of the few specific studies that have been developed which shows the value of long-range planning; in fact long-range planning is so new in American business that insufficient time has gone by for any tangible evidence to exist as to the real value of long-range planning. Notwithstanding the lack of evidence as to the value of long-range planning, there is little doubt logically as to how valuable a technique it is in business. In the author's opinion several valuable by-products can be derived from the long-range planning effort.

1. Crystallization of executive thinking is more likely to take place if long-range planners are expected to produce long-range recommendations and especially if such recommendations are to be put in writing.

2. The long-range planning committee investigations are an excellent means of keeping top executives informed about different parts of the business.

3. Planning for the long-term may disclose blind spots and potential problem areas which the regular management group might easily miss in a rapidly expanding firm.

4. The long-range planning group can provide a company-wide sounding board for appraising the potential of new techniques.

5. Long-range planning provides an excellent opportunity to evaluate management personnel; particularly it facilitates an evaluation of divisional managers in the decentralized situation.

6. Long-range planning provides a medium for latent ideas and talent which might never have reached the open because there was no appropriate moment in the rush of daily operations.

7. By establishing company goals, objectives, and policies for long-range planning the organizational structure of the company is stabilized and strengthened but yet has an inherent flexibility to expand or contract as needed in order to support developing markets.

8. The existence of a formal long-range planning philosophy improves communication and coordination within the business by providing a standard against which all activity can be compared and motivated.

9. One of the greatest by-products of long-range planning is that the planner and all management groups supporting him are forced to consider problems and opportunities concurrently and to find the best solution instead of the most expedient one. The study of abstract problems in relationship to each other lends a perspective that enables the executive to direct his efforts more effectively.

In the experience of companies that have done long-range planning it has these advantages:

1. It guides management in conforming every-day company decision and action to overall company philosophy and objectives.

2. It provides a framework for the chief executive in planning the company's future.

3. It provides a guide for addition or deletion of products.

4. It guides personnel recruitment, training and development.

5. It serves as a background for financial control.

6. It serves as a morale builder for the younger management group.

7. It develops the habit of organized thinking and planning at all levels of management.[28]

Long-range planning delineates the requirements for maintaining or enlarging a competitive position within an already established market. By visualizing the future and evaluating the results of long-range planning the requirements for additional capital and the timing thereof are clearly indicated. The fact that a company has a long-range plan considerably strengthens its position in seeking new capital; not only the acquisition of capital is facilitated but the need for specific personnel will be apparent in sufficient time to recruit or train efficiently. In addition a stable base on which to plan current operations evolves with the result that short-term fluctuations do not color operating decisions out of proportion to their overall importance.

Long-range planning provides the means to keep abreast of dynamic markets, a particularly important consideration in consumer-oriented industries; overall market objectives can be tied to specific production, research, finance and sales plans with a resulting balanced effort among all facets of the company's operation. In addition a very real benefit of long-range planning is that it provides a medium for the objective evaluation of company progress through the periodic evaluation of the external and internal factors affecting a company's weaknesses and strengths.

The foregoing paragraphs have reflected but a few of the direct and indirect benefits of long-range planning; the list could be multiplied in an almost endless fashion. All of these benefits appear to be

---

[28]"Plan Tomorrow's Profits", Nation's Business (August, 1958), p. 76.

directed towards the reduction of ad hoc management through the establishment of specific operating plans to achieve long-range objectives.
By making use of a wide range of statistics, trade information, research
and development, economic indicators, and the many other facets of long-
range planning a company is better able to predict the future. By predicting this future and then planning for it a business is in a better
position to cope with that future when it arrives.

Long-range planning can make the difference between business prosperity and failure in future years. It is a philosophy under which management can operate to give a company a major competitive advantage.
Comprehensive planning attempts to achieve a consistent, coordinated
structure of operations focused on desired ends. Business decisions
flow naturally from such planned activity. The further the planning
goes into the future the more flexible it must be. Planning facilitates
control for by setting standards in advance day-to-day progress can be
more easily evaluated and tested. One of the greatest results of long-
range planning is that it gives management confidence about the future.
As noted by Payne:

> I think that one of the most important concepts of forward plan-
> ning is that it does not assume there will be ideal business
> conditions or "smooth sailing." Unexpected things will happen
> -- gyrations in the market or the loss of a key man -- but they
> in no way affect the practicality of planning. As a matter of
> fact, one of the values of a good long-term program is that it
> helps to keep executives from panicking when reverses happen or
> dips occur.[29]

The contribution of long-range planning to the high growth rate of a company is indicated in a study conducted by the Stanford Research Institute

---

[29]Bruce Payne, "Steps In Long-Range Planning," Harvard Business
Review (March-April, 1957), p. 104.

in 1955. According to this study an element of a successful company is
a forward-looking program to promote its future in such areas as product
development, market development, company acquisitions, organization or
management development and operations research. Companies that have
grown rapidly have given evidence of supporting future growth programs
through such means as long-range company planning, product research and
development, market research, diversification into other product fields
and markets and acquisition of other companies.[30] Companies with formalized planning programs appear to be enthusiastic about their value.
Many consider long-range forecasting and planning absolutely essential
to sustain the growth rate that is sought.

Perhaps the most commonly recognized result of long-range planning
is that it provides a framework for the tactical guidance of existing
operations. However, it has another important and relatively unfamiliar
advantage to offer. According to Hill and Granger: "As a strategic tool,
it enables a company to develop entirely new concepts and areas of operation.[31]

Some organizational changes and departmental realignments have
resulted as a direct influence of long-range planning activities, especially since World War II. Notwithstanding the absence of specific
changes or results a real benefit from long-range planning has been the
improved performance of a company as measured by a return on investment
or by the accomplishment of the service objective and the orderly and

---

[30]N. R. Maines, Why Companies Grow (Menlo Park, California: Stanford Research Institute, 1957), p. 4.

[31]William E. Hill and Charles H. Granger, "Charting Your Company's
Future Growth," Dun's Review and Modern Industry (August, 1957), p. 43.

complete discharge of the organization's social and ethical responsibilities to the local and national community. Some of the results of long-
range planning are not directly traceable per se and are reflected in
better morale and improved local performance. By requiring daily application it continually provides a practical training program for junior
management; the very existence of a comprehensive long-range plan, properly founded and documented, is excellent evidence to present of growth
opportunities to a lender during credit negotiations. It provides the
means for the development of new and better ways to meet customer requirements.

Principal Elements in the Contemporary Philosophy
of Long-Range Planning

The period 1940 through 1950 had seen the realization on the part
of business of the necessity for a long-term planning capability in order
to meet changing economic, technological, and political factors within
the competitive environment. It was during the contemporary period that
scholars and practitioners synthesized the philosophical framework of
long-range planning. Long-range planning became envisioned as an intellectual process requiring reflective thinking which placed greater
premium on the conceptual skills of executive management than did any
other phase of top management. Looked at diagrammatically, a corporation's long-range planning process appeared as a vast group of interrelationships between short-term and long-term marketing, production,
and financial phenomena; all planning was predicated on certain premises
and assumptions established from a comprehensive analysis and evaluation
of the internal and external environment in which the company operates.

Contemporary literature and thinking had not developed a classic definition of long-range planning; some scholars attempted to define it in
terms of time, others as related to the breadth of the corporate planning
effort, and still others described it as a process whose time dimensions
resulted from the peculiarities of the functional area of consideration.

By 1960 it was recognized by most respondent companies that modern
long-range planning, as a science that had fully emerged in the contemporary period, played an important role in making the economic situation
in the United States more stable than it had ever been before. Long-range
planning concepts stressed the thought that individual business units,
managed by a rational, informed being, were capable of formulating plans
and realizing long-term objectives without the aid of a central government coordinating agency. Although the existing philosophy of long-range
planning incorporates a wholly national and pragmatic outlook, it might
be well to indicate that an institutional mind beyond the capabilities
of any single planner operates for a directed combination of individual
plans which lead toward an overall national goal of economic stability.
From the viewpoint of the industry as a whole, increasing intervention
on the part of government and the survival of the economic system that
permits private enterprise may very well depend on the economic stability
that results from such system; long-range planning appeared during contemporary times as the nearest thing to a panacea that could prevent another depression such as occurred in the 1930's. It is not at all clear
that the economic system of the United States could survive another such
depression without traumatic social and political changes.

Comprehensive long-term business planning came into its own largely
since the second World War but more especially since the period 1950 to

the present. The next stage of emphasis and development will be the improvement of existing methods and techniques of planning. In time corporate long-range planning will become so widespread and used in companies of all sizes that corporate planners will turn increasingly to game
theory and other tools to optimize strategic planning in order to meet
competition. For large corporations there will be more staff positions
created which are specifically devoted to long-range planning.

Contemporary writers began looking for a relationship between company long-range planning and growth; however, long-range planning is not
presented as a panacea for all company ills, as some large and successful
companies have demonstrated an innate ability to detect and adjust to
change without any apparent formal long-range procedures or processes.
Some managements are seemingly effective in uncovering and evaluating
investable opportunities without any more long-range planning than is
done on an informal basis by executive personnel in the normal decision
making process. The odds, however, for corporate growth have appeared
highest when the top executives are imbued with a long-range planning
philosophy and constantly apply long-run criteria to their day-to-day
decision making and use their long-range plans as a strategic goal around
which to plan operational activities.

Although a high percentage of respondents is engaged in long-range
planning, the present study indicates that not all companies are so engaged. Some contemporary literature reporting on similar studies supports this observation. Notwithstanding the absence of complete support
to long-range planning by contemporary businesses, however, there has
appeared a definite pattern of principal elements of the contemporary
philosophy:

1. Long-range planning is recognized as a proprietary function and responsibility of top management although separate staff agencies are being appointed to assist line managers in this function. Long-range planning became identified as an evolving differentiated organic function of management.

2. Long-range planning is carried on by the institutional mind of the organization and as such exists as an intellectual process and concept beyond the frame of reference of any single executive in the organization. As contemplated by the institutional mind long-range planning pervades all functional and ancillary areas of the organization and exists as a basing point for operational matters.

3. Long-range planning is not forecasting but is necessary because one cannot forecast; it identifies the proper risks that must be assumed by the management. Long-range planning is not an entity in itself; its primary purpose is to provide the guidelines necessary for the decision-making processes throughout the organization.

4. Causal factors initiating the requirement for long-range planning include internal and external factors. Company growth and complexity, diverse production activities, and increasingly complex technology are cited as intra-company factors: competitive elements, availability of planning tools, union influences, social factors, government influences and elements of the managerial environment have all influenced the company from an extra-organizational point of view.

5. The majority of business firms doing long-range planning take into consideration the possibility of a serious downturn in business activity as evidenced by the preparation of long-term plans which contemplate contraction of operations as well as expansion plans.

6. There appears to be a trend to the creation of a master long-range plan for individual company use. Long-range planning is carried on as a continuous effort in the majority of the companies. Long-range planning is not accomplished without difficulties and limitations although most of such problems are attributable to factors, forces, and activities which are within the jurisdiction of corporate management. Extra-organizational difficulties, such as government controls, business cycle influences and industry peculiarities play a relatively minor role.

7. The overall corporate long-range planning period is that time dimension in which the necessary functional and additional areas of effort are planned so as to provide for an orderly and efficient employment of the factors of production in the accomplishment of the organizational service objective with relation to a specific corporate goal. The planning period becomes primarily a function of the functional area of effort under consideration. Complex factors determine the planning period; some of the most important are industry peculiarities, market demand, availability of resources, the lead time involved in the product life cycle, and the specific objectives of the corporation. While there appears to be somewhat arbitrary selection of planning periods some uniformity exists between the planning periods of the major functional areas of effort.

8. Contemporary scholars and practitioners support the idea of a high degree of participation in long-range planning by all line executive personnel; there is a definite objection to using management consultants to do the long-range planning for a firm although considerable use is made of consultants to provide specific information and guidance for the planning. Two serious objections are raised to using consultants

to do all of the planning, viz., whereas a consultant does the work he and not the company gets the experience; and, the personnel in the company doing a particular kind of work have a real background of the company, its problems and its approach to doing business that cannot be expected of an outsider, however capable.

9. Existing organizational frameworks for long-range planning vary widely in practice but there is evidence that they are all based on rather conventional ideas. Most of the companies established a specific organizational entity for long-range planning subsequent to World War II and especially since 1950. The individual in charge of long-range planning is a top management official; before establishing a specific long-range planning agency, this activity was performed by ad hoc task groups, executive committees, or by a top executive as an additional duty.

10. Composition of contemporary long-range planning staffs, by professional areas of effort, reflect a breadth and depth of technical capability. Management and marketing personnel are reported most frequently on the long-range planning staff. The providing of economic data in the absence of a staff is accomplished in a multitude of ways such as by trade associations, by attendance at professional meetings, and by perusal of contemporary literature.

11. Cooperating companies indicate that there are few functions which are not subject to planning on a long-term basis. The emphasis on long-range planning varies according to the significance of the different activities in each corporation. The organic functions of business are considered of top importance by contemporary companies engaged in long-range planning.

12. Economic factors play an important part in the development of meaningful plans for a company's future. Contemporary businesses consider a broad base of economic phenomena affecting the company's future. From an aggregate standpoint industry trends and competitor's actions are cited most frequently as prime extra-organizational economic considerations of long-range planning.

13. Most companies enter into some degree of long-range planning before establishing long-term objectives. The long-range planning process itself has internal objectives apart from the overall company goals.

14. Techniques used by industry to pretest its plans vary from the use of formal decision laboratories where computers and models are used to informal testing accomplished by the exercise of executive judgment. The principal method thus far, and the one which seems to pervade all areas, is management judgment. There are presently no all-encompassing models in operations research that can be relied on to evaluate overall company long-range planning.

15. Contemporary thinking about long-range planning recognizes primary and ancillary benefits to be derived from such planning; the greatest value stems from the fact that business is better prepared to meet the uncertain future by providing a framework for the tactical guidance of existing operations. Contemporary companies report that organizational, product, and other changes have come about directly as a result of long-range planning. New product lines and product diversification have been the principal tangible results of long-range planning.

16. The emergence of long-range planning as a differentiated function of management has concurrently resulted in the development of specific procedures and techniques designed to effect long-range plan-

ning within the framework of an existing management philosophy. Contemporary writers began conceiving of long-range planning as a series of basic inter-related steps proceeding in orderly fashion from the establishment of long-term objectives to the actual implementation of a plan. The study conducted by the author, while recognizing that these general steps do exist, does not accept them as necessarily all encompassing; the major steps pursued become a function of many variables such as the type of business, industry demand, product mix, and the desires and capabilities of the executives doing the actual planning. Contemporary thinking does recognize the need for the development of refined techniques and procedures; recency of any wide application of long-range planning to American business precludes any full scale development of standard operating procedures. These will doubtlessly be developed in the next decade. Coordination of long-range plans; reviewing and validating existing plans; increasing forecasting capabilities; improving the use of long-range planning tools; and other methodology in long-range planning provides contemporary management with challenges for the future.

By the end of 1961 long-range planning had emerged as a fairly well differentiated function of management. As a philosophy it pervades the organizational structure of a large percentage of the large American businesses studied and provides a framework from which general corporate activities are conducted. The framework of principles, ideas and practices of long-range planning are given an identifiable separateness and unity of their own; a rational effort had been made to answer the questions of the widest generality conceivable posed about it. Out of this developed a body of belief and practice aimed at achieving better performance. The philosophy of long-range planning had emerged by 1960;

future years promised to broaden the existing philosophy particularly
in terms of developing more sophisticated procedures and techniques.
Long-range planning became conceived of as risk-taking decision making;
the systematic organization of the planning job and the supply of knowledge to it portended more effective managerial qualities and more efficient employment of the factors of production.

CHAPTER VI

SUMMARY AND CONCLUSIONS

Summary

The recent attention given long-range planning in management literature aroused the author's interest in tracing the origin and development of a philosophy of long-range planning in American business. In
the introductory part of the study it was necessary to discuss the development of a philosophy and to establish the criteria for the essential
elements and framework of the philosophy; later portions of the study
were devoted to a comprehensive analysis and examination of historical
and contemporary thought and practice on long-range planning to see if
long-range planning did evolve into a philosophy in the contemporary
world. In tracing this evolving philosophy long-range planning was derived as a fairly well differentiated organic function of management,
conceived and developed from an existing philosophy of management. Material for identifying the historical derivation of long-range planning
came primarily from a scrutiny of published periodical and book literature. A comprehensive review of pertinent literature extending back to
1885 was undertaken in order to isolate and study the beginning written
thoughts about long-range planning; military literature was examined in
great detail inasmuch as it was an early and prolific source of long-
range planning thought. Both historical and contemporary literature
were found to be lacking in an integrated study of long-range planning.
In the author's extensive research no evidence was found of any attempt
to trace the evolving philosophy of long-range planning nor was any
study found which satisfied the author's requirement for a contemporary

philosophy. Consequently it became necessary to resort to primary re-search in order to glean the pertinent qualitative and quantitative data for the study; accordingly an extensive questionnaire was developed, tested, and dispatched to a select group of contemporary American busi-nesses.

The breadth of the subject necessitated the imposition of certain strict limitations insofar as possible; consequently the study was not concerned with:

1. Short-range planning;

2. Businesses not falling into the 500 largest American businesses reflected in The Fortune Directory;

3. Specific computer, linear programming, mathematical, statisti-cal, and econometric techniques and processes. However, the general use of such tools in long-range planning was broached;

4. Periods prior to 1885 except as some military long-range plan-ning was concerned;

5. The full development of long-range planning by functional area of effort; rather the study was concerned with long-range planning as an overall corporate activity.

The military evolution of the general staff concept and its conse-quent role in military long-range planning was examined in Chapter II; such a study served to lay the basis for a discussion of the influence that military long-range planning has had on American business. The military establishment, as presently organized, emphasizes long-range planning in its activities. The historical examples available in mili-tary literature showed the advantage of military long-range planning; the contemporary general staff exists primarily to effect long-term planning.

The early development of a philosophy of long-range planning in American business was reported in Chapter III; the framework of thought about long-range planning was developed based upon the following organization:

1. Early long-range planning rudiments (1880-1900).

2. Evolution of long-range planning images (1900-1930).

3. Recognition of the need for long-range planning in American business (1930-1940).

4. The expansion of long-range planning concepts (1940-1950). In discussing the early development initial attention was given to the derivation of a planning concept as reflected in management literature; early examples of long-range planning were reflected and discussed. Corollary to the discussion of long-range planning the economic and industrial climate of the period was examined in order to relate such conditions to the evolving philosophy of long-range planning. Early pioneers and their contributions were reviewed and discussed; special care was taken to excerpt the singular and infrequent references to long-range planning as expounded by scholars and practitioners of the period. The influence of national economic planning on individual business planning and the growing influence of management literature on long-range planning was evaluated.

Chapters IV and V were concerned with the contemporary philosophy of long-range planning in American business. The material discussed in these chapters was a reflection of the input and conclusions derived from the questionnaire received from participating companies; in addition the parallel thought of contemporary writers was presented along with the primary data in order to give structure and depth to the evolving philos-

ophy. The relationship of long-range planning in terms of its purpose
and definition to the top management hierarchy was reviewed; the derivation of the need for long-range planning, the extent of long-range planning in large American business and the difficulties of long-range planning evaluated. Planning period determinants, organization for long-range
planning and the functional areas of long-range planning were reviewed.
An analysis of the influence of extra-organizational factors and some of
the procedures and techniques for long-range planning were afforded.
Finally a look at possible future innovations was given and the principal
elements in the contemporary philosophy of long-range planning were identified and discussed. Contemporary thinking on long-range planning recognizes it as a fairly well differentiated function of management.

The last chapter of the paper was devoted to a summary and conclusion of the study effort and the major findings thereof.

Findings

The term long-range planning has appeared on a recurring basis
only recently in management literature; however early mention of the
term can be traced back to pre-depression days. American business in
the post-war period has become more concerned with long-range planning
procedures and techniques in order to prepare better for the future.
Contemporary studies in long-range planning lack the depth and comprehensiveness required to determine if a philosophy of long-range planning exists in present management thinking.

Influence of Military Establishment

A strong influence was found to have been exerted by military
thinking on the subject of long-range planning; the general staff was

organized primarily to effect long-range planning in the military establishment. The influence of the military staff has been significant in
the business world; the military general staff was found to have had its
inception in antiquity. A contemporary general staff exists primarily
as a staff planning and supervising agency, not as an agency for operations.
Contemporary general staff organization and employment is based on the refinement given it by the German General Staff. The success of the German
General Staff, as a peace-time planning center, is manifest in the employment of the plans that this staff developed during the Franco-Prussian
wars and the First and Second World Wars.

The development of military long-range planning concepts is believed to have closely paralleled the evolving philosophy of the employment of a military staff agency. However, the nature of primitive staff
long-range planning is veiled in obscurity; long-range planning in the
military sense seems to have developed out of logistic planning whose
time dimensions became greater as the campaigns became more complex and
extended over wide geographical areas. In modern times general staff
planning is projected many years into the future and plans are formulated
which encompass total commitment of a nation's resources. There is evidence that the military concept of long-range planning was widely used by
military groups long before such an image was recognized and developed in
the business world. The most probable reason for this, at least in the
United States, is that prior to contemporary times, a strong popular feeling has existed that military people are necessarily rigid and incompetent; Taylor seems to have had a distrust of military forms of organization as evidenced by his development of functional foremanship as a replacement for the military form of organization. The total requirements

of waging World War II on a global basis, however, motivated a closer relationship of the military and civilian components of the United States
society; any form of distrust of military organization or methods was
subordinated to the overall demanding requirements for rapid production
of the materials of war. At this point industry saw the need for the development of a philosophy of long-range planning.

Whatever may have caused businessmen to neglect an early acceptance
of the military philosophy of long-range planning is debatable; however,
the concept of long-range planning is a birthright of the military, both
in inception and employment.

Early Planning Images

Planning is recognized by most authorities as an organic function
of management; historical literature reflects an abundance of thought on
short-range planning with conceptualization occurring around the turn of
the present century. Early industrial leaders manifested a type of informal and executive long-range planning as evidenced by the combinations
and consolidations of industrial power which occurred in the late nineteenth century. Management literature changed significantly during the
twentieth century; in the early period management groups and scholars
paid attention to management problems at the shop level and neglected
somewhat the administrative or general management of the enterprise.
Henri Fayol's observations on the principles of general management exerted a strong influence in later periods; Fayol placed considerable emphasis on the managerial function of prevoyance and developed a concept
of long-range planning in his writings relative to the drawing up of a
plan of action in a large mining and metallurgical firm. The period

1900-1930 provided ample opportunity in terms of the economic environment for the evolution of long-range planning images. Several writers
attempted to relate the organizational service objective of a business
and the business's future. Planning was conceived of as an organic function but received relatively little attention in the development of time
dimensions thereof.

Influence of the Depression Years

Early periods of the depression of the thirties fostered an abundance of thinking on national economic planning as a panacea to prevent
another costly depression in the American economy; a few scholars and
businessmen developed a counter movement to the strong social-economic
planning by supporting the idea that business planning done individually
would in the aggregate provide high productivity and contribute to the
general social security and well-being of the society more than would a
strong form of centralized government planning. Trade associations
facilitated corporate long-range planning; in fact literature in 1931
specifically enjoined them to provide leadership in this area.

Urgencies of the immediate business situation in the depressed
thirties forced many managers to resort to expediency instead to planned
policies on long-range planning. Some recognition, however, was given
to the need for long-range planning based on the long-term trends of
certainty. Scholars in the first half of the 1930's sought a combined
social, political, and economic solution to the prostrate economy;
academicians and a few enlightened business leaders began to speak and
write of the long-term responsibilities of business leaders. A few industry leaders began to write and tell of individual company planning

techniques for long-term considerations; these leaders recognized the need for long-range planning but failed to develop any integrated functional approach to the task.

Influence of the Period 1940-1950

The industrial and economic climate of the forties was significantly influenced by World War II. Preparation and conduct of a global war called for unprecedented industrial and military expansion and cooperation. Management of an organization under a philosophy which neglected the long-run considerations became untenable in terms of society's demands for economic security. Concurrently with the evolution of long-range planning concepts in the period 1940-1950 there arose an acceptance of the role of the governmental, economic, and social planner in the contemporary world. The requirement for long-term planning for post-war markets caused much of the ill repute in which planning had recently been held to disappear; and the heads of corporations, labor leaders, and governmental agencies, all began to acknowledge the need for a concept of planning.

Many industry leaders, motivated by the requirement for post-war planning, appointed an organizational entity or an individual on part-time duty to study the future of the company. Specific attention was given to the problem of peace-time conversion of existing facilities and organizational structures. The emergence of a new and seemingly permanent function of long-range planning was not without difficulties; lack of data and trained personnel were the most vexing.

Growing management literature of the twentieth century, which placed more emphasis on the role of the top management group for planning the future of the business doubtlessly exerted a strong influence on the development of a philosophy of long-range planning. More and more top

level businessmen began to evaluate critically their role in the organization and in so doing delegated many of the immediate operating problems
to their staff agencies; with this delegation the top management group
had sufficient time to give more thought to the long-term trends of their
concerns and in so doing recognized the inadequacy of their organization's
preparation for the future. Consequently they initiated a long-range
planning effort within the organization.

Effects of Contemporary Thinking on Long-Range Planning

By 1950 the idea of long-range planning was still a concept in
the minds of individuals within the organization; the evolving philosophy
was not sufficiently developed to be conceived by the institutional mind
of the enterprise or in terms of experience larger than that which came
to any one individual. The evolving concepts were broadened in scope
and depth; a refinement and revaluation of techniques and procedures was
attempted. Some integration of the functional element of long-range
planning was effected.

By 1950 the term long-range planning was appearing more frequently
in business literature; during this period the philosophical synthesis
of long-range planning was effected. Literature of the period emphasized
the need for top management to delegate the operational aspects of the
business to subordinates and concentrate on planning for the future. An
intimate relationship existed between top management and long-range planning.

No standard and comprehensive definition of long-range planning
had been formulated; it is not, however, an entity in itself as its primary purpose is to provide the guide lines necessary for vital decision
making throughout the organization.

As might be expected not all companies agree that long-range planning was possible or necessary; volatile labor conditions, frequent price changes, cyclical demands, unstable consumer preference and government control are cited as reasons for not effecting long-range planning. However, an overwhelming majority of the participating companies indicate that long-range planning was being accomplished. Company growth and complexity, diverse production activities, long lead times for product development, and the trend toward decentralization are some of the internal reasons for developing a long-range planning capability. External factors which created the need for long-range planning include competitive elements, availability of planning tools, union influences, social factors, changing technology in product development, and the optimistic belief by industry leaders in the ability of the individual company and the economy to grow. A complex inter-relationship of many factors, forces, and effects stimulated the growth of long-range planning. Most of the long-range planning was initiated in the period 1950-1961. The establishment of the initial long-range planning effort was approached in a variety of ways; most companies depended solely on the creative ability of company personnel rather than on outside assistance. There was a definite emphasizing of participation in the long-range planning process as a fundamental way of gaining middle and lower management support. Most of the companies did long-term planning which included the development of contraction of operations as well as expansion. There was a trend toward the creation of a master long-range plan for individual company use. Long-range planning was a continuous effort in the majority of the companies

studied but was not done without difficulties and limitations. Major
limitations and difficulties include --

1. Lack of sufficient data;

2. External business factors that cannot be anticipated accurately;

3. Business cycle influences;

4. Industry peculiarities.

Most difficulties are attributable to factors, forces, and activities
which are within the jurisdiction of the corporate management. Extra-
organizational difficulties appear to play a minor role. Contemporary
writers also recognize certain difficulties and limitations to the long-
range planning process.

The planning period for long-range planning must be approached in
a variety of ways with two of the main considerations being the functional
area of effort and that time dimension in which the necessary functional
and additional areas of effort are planned; a series of complex factors
determines the period of the planning effort. Major functional and additional areas of effort among companies reflect a similarity of planning period. Evidence seems to indicate that there should be some logic
in selecting the right time range for a company's planning; in all probability a company should not plan for a period longer than is economically
justifiable.

Management literature is reflecting a growing realization that
good long-range planning must proceed both up and down the organizational
structure. While organizational frameworks for long-range planning vary
widely in practice, there is some evidence that they are based on rather
conventional ideas. No stereotyped rules exist to follow in the organization of the planning group since each company must use the individual

advantages inherent in its own organization. Most of the cooperating companies established a specific organizational entity for long-range planning subsequent to 1950. Individuals in charge of long-range planning are located at a high level in the organization. There is a tendency to move from the use of a committee for long-range planning toward a long-range planning office, although most long-range planning offices are staffed by a relatively small group of people; composition of the long-range planning staffs reflect a breadth and depth of technical and professional capability. Management and marketing personnel are reported most frequently on the long-range planning staff. Companies seek assistance and information from consultants; however, many objections to using outside agencies to do the long-range planning were cited.

Cooperating companies indicate that in general there are few functions which are not subject to some planning on a long-term basis. Not every field of activity is planned in every company; even between companies in the same industry there are differences in the period for which long-range plans are formulated.

Economic factors play an important part in the development of meaningful plans for a company's future. Such factors as the general level of prosperity in the country, population growth, changes in consumer spending patterns, technological changes, new competitive products, and a host of other factors must be identified and evaluated as part of the long-range planning process. The influence of the economic factors is a function of the type of business engaged in.

Most companies appear to enter into some long-range planning before establishing long-term objectives. Pretesting of long-range plans is a difficult task and in practice varies from the use of formal decision laboratories to the informal "mental testing" done by a manager when he approves a phase in the formulation of a plan. The principal method thus far, and the one which seems to pervade all areas, is management judgment. Many other diverse means are used; contemporary literature is almost devoid of writings on the subject of pretesting long-range plans.

Several primary and ancillary results occur from long-range planning. The greatest value is that the business engaged in long-range planning is better prepared to meet the uncertain future and to assume the right risks. Planning provides a framework for the tactical guidance of existing operations. Specific organizational, product, and other changes have come about directly as a result of long-range planning. Several alternative methods exist for communicating the plan to those responsible for implementing it.

The emergence of the long-range planning function in business has initiated the requirement for the development of concurrent procedures and techniques devised to effect the long-range planning within the framework of an existing management philosophy. The long-range planning process, as composed of procedures and techniques, varies from company to company. The development of procedures and techniques is a purposeful responsibility that cannot be delegated to subordinates although they may participate. A big factor in developing procedures is to provide for the coordination of the long-range planning. Normal intra-staff coordination predominates as the method used in most of the companies as the vehicle through which the long-range planning is coordinated. The review and updating of plans is an essential part of the coordination function. Most plans are reviewed on an annual basis.

Forecasting in long-range planning is recognized as the projecting of future economic, legislative, and technological factors of the economy and the relation of such factors to the company's future posture. Many forecasts are made which range from sales forecasts to attempts at predicting the social mores of certain of the customers. The degree of participation by cooperating companies indicates that considerable management attention has been focused on this activity. Other tools used in long-range planning are still the traditional ones which have been developed in other phases of the business. As future planning becomes more sophisticated some of the newer techniques, such as game theory, model construction, input-output theory will be refined. Use of the many planning tools does not negate the requirement for the continued exercise of management judgment.

Many future innovations in long-range planning can be expected; a paramount refinement will be the integration of long-range planning with higher manager development; other innovations center around the collection and interpretation of planning data and the organization for long-range planning activity.

In the period 1950-1960 long-range planning became conceived as an intellectual process requiring reflective thinking which placed great premium on the conceptual skills of management. A company's long-range planning became a comprehensive array of internal and external factors and forces whose mastery significantly affected the individual business's future. The principal elements of both contemporary and historical periods will be reflected in the conclusions.

Conclusions

Long-range planning, as an activity arising from the organic function of planning, had its early development in the military establishment. Concepts of long-range planning existed in business circles before businessmen and scholars began writing about it; within the military organization its origin can be traced back to antiquity. Basic differentiation of long-range planning from operations or short-term planning centers around the time dimensions thereof and the internal and external organizational considerations evaluated in the institutional mind of the business organization.

How to perpetuate the growth of a business unit and concurrently provide a service to its customers is one of the chief aims of scientific management. Contemporary thinking on the subject of long-range planning leads one to the conclusion that much can be done to insure a business's future through the medium of long-range planning. As would be expected the contemporary philosophy of long-range planning did not develop in a vacuum but rather evolved as the product of environmental factors, forces, and effects. How that philosophy arose and what its elemental framework is will be concluded in this section. Concluding remarks will follow the organization of the study.

1. Military leaders developed line and staff concepts long before such ideas were accepted by business.

The general staff was created primarily as a long-range planning agency; the military establishment, with its refinement and employment of long-range plans significantly influenced long-range planning in American business. That military planners have been effective has been demon-

strated by the successful planning efforts of World War II and more recently in the development and employment of the Polaris and other missile
systems.

Business is indebted to the military for much in the way of concepts,
techniques, and methodology in the matter of long-range planning. The
birthright for long-range planning must be given to the military general
staff.

2. Development of early long-range planning rudiments occurred
in the period 1880-1900.

The seeds of management thought as to long-range planning started
to germinate during the last decade of the nineteenth century. Business
literature during this period is devoid of specific references to long-
range planning; rudiments of long-range planning, however, did exist and
were manifested in the actions of the industrial and business combinations
and mergers of the period.

3. Evolution of long-range planning images occurred in the period
1900-1930.

Management scholars began to classify the profession and differentiate the organic functions thereof. Time dimensions were first applied
to business planning. The period provided ample opportunity in terms of
the economic environment for the evaluation of long-range planning images.

Fayol contributed the most significant writing on long-range planning. His recognition of the importance of prevoyance and his forecasting
techniques were extraordinary contributions for his time.

Long-range planning was recognized as a rudiment; however, no attempt was made to develop procedures and techniques. Long-range planning

as a fairly well differentiated function of management existed in the mental images of some leaders as a business necessity; however American business failed to develop any real appreciation for the philosophical possibilities of such an activity.

4. In the period 1930-1940 businessmen recognized the need for long-range planning in American business.

Although businessmen in general lost prestige in the public eye the career manager arose; serious consideration was given to the long-term responsibilities of business leaders.

Politicians, business leaders, economists, and industrialists recognized the need for long-range planning as a possible counter-force to the recessions and depressions which had plagued the nation. Long-range planning was conceptualized only in the individual minds of corporate management.

5. The expansion of long-range planning concepts occurred in the period 1940-1950.

Close cooperation between many segments of the society facilitated the common pursuit of the global war. The military establishment during this period exerted a profound and continuing influence on the national economy.

Inquiries concerning business objectives served to focus attention on the top management function of planning. Individual company management groups visualized their business as a segment of a larger economy operated according to some social and economic plan.

Evolving concepts of long-range planning were broadened in scope and depth and refinements and re-evaluation of techniques and procedures was attempted. Some integration of the functional elements of long-range planning was accomplished.

6. A mature philosophy of long-range planning in American business was developed in the era 1950-1961

It was during this period that long-range planning became envisioned as a distinct intellectual process and encompassed a vast group of interrelationships of the elements of the business organization and its environment. Long-range planning became predicated on certain premises and assumptions established from a comprehensive analysis and evaluation of the internal and external environment in which the company operated. Contemporary thought had not, however, developed a classic definition of long-range planning.

Long-range planning was contemplated by the institutional mind of the corporation which was a mind beyond the capabilities of a single planner and operated for a directed combination of individual plans which lead to an overall national goal of economic stability. Long-range planning came into its own largely since World War II.

A high percentage of the large American businesses surveyed are engaged in long-range planning; a few, however, appear successful without claiming to do any long-range planning.

Long-range planning became recognized as a fairly well differentiated function of management. Specific procedures and techniques have been developed for conducting long-range planning; future innovations will be effected in long-range planning as the state of the art advances. A philosophy of long-range planning pervades the organizational structure of a high percentage of businesses surveyed and thereby provides a framework from which general company activities are conducted.

7. The existing philosophy of long-range planning is composed of a framework of principles, ideas, and concepts which are given an identifiable separateness and unity of their own.

Contemporary writers have made a rational effort to answer every conceivable question about long-range planning.

Out of the thinking and writing of twentieth century management literature has arisen a body of belief and practices about long-range planning aimed at achieving better performance.

Recommendations

Knowledge gained in the study leads to recommendations that should be made for a firm that is contemplating the establishment of a long-range planning activity. Initially it is urged that any long-range planning effort spring naturally from an established philosophy of management; long-range planning is so vital to insuring a firm's future that it must be wholeheartedly supported by top management and at all other executive levels throughout the organization. Specific recommendations akin to the establishment of a long-range planning effort are:

1. The organizational location of the long-range planning office is of paramount importance; it is recommended that it report to the top management level, preferably the president or the executive vice president. Such a reporting position in the organizational hierarchy will insure the fullest exercise of authority and responsibility in order to plan, organize, and control the long-range planning effort throughout the company. Care should be exercised to differentiate between **line** and **staff** responsibilities and authorities essential to long-range planning; specific duties

should be spelled out in a company policy manual. It is urged that the creation of a long-range planning office not reduce the amount of subordinate line and staff participation in the development of organizational plans.

2. The long-range planning staff should be composed of those personnel skills necessary to provide technical and facilitative support to the long-range planning effort. The specific type of professional and technical skills depends to some degree on the type of business, however certain professional representation is required such as economists, statisticians, managers, marketeers, production specialists, and financial managers. In the event personnel austerity precludes the assignment of full-time specialists from these areas, part-time participation should be required. In any event specific coverage should be given to insure that all economic, technological, and legislative factors affecting the company's future are identified and analyzed by the planning staff. It is recommended that consideration be given to the establishment of a market intelligence service similar in general duties and organization to the intelligence officer on the military staff. In the event certain information is required infrequently or is of a highly specialized nature, it may be more economical to contract for the services of a professional economist; it is recommended that special care be exercised to insure that any consultants used do not impinge on the prerogatives and responsibilities of company executives.

3. It is urged that the master plan be developed which provides the future parameters around which the company proposes to operate. The master plan should include the overall corporate goals as well as ancil-

lary objectives for corporate sub-divisions; every functional area and facet of company activity conducive to long-range planning should be included and portrayed in a time phasing relationship. Such a plan must be distributed to all executives who have a responsibility for implementing a portion of it; it should be a living document under recurring review as to currency, comprehensiveness, and company supportability. It is recommended that objectives for corporate and sub-division be established after sufficient long-range planning is accomplished in order to determine feasibility, practicality, and supportability of corporate goals.

4. It is recommended that the corporate long-range planning period that is established take into consideration the appropriate corporate area of effort. It is urged that the overall corporate planning period be constructed so that the commitment of resources necessary to attain the attendant objectives are controllable and predictable. A company should plan as far ahead as is useful but only so far as it is possible to do so with reasonable accuracy. The type of business engaged in, the availability of resources, the expected competitive situations, and the temperament of the management are a few of the factors that should be considered in establishing long-range planning periods.

5. Company personnel should be required to recognize that the planning for long-term considerations is a formidable task; consequently concerned executives must be prepared to recognize the real existence of difficulties and limitations. Inasmuch as most of the limitations and difficulties are well within the company framework, it is urged that aggressive and continued management improvement be effected to remove the long-range planning interferences.

6. The establishment of long-range planning suggests that specific steps for the conduct of such an activity can be formulated; long-range planning, as a management function should be planned, organized, controlled and carried on as a continuous effort in the corporate structure. Specific procedures and techniques must be established through maximum participation of executives and should be continually evaluated and improved as the state of the art in long-range planning advances in the company. Tools should be developed which facilitate the long-range planning effort; however, executives are enjoined to exercise care to temper the long-range planning tools with prudent judgment.

7. It is recommended that provisions be made for the pretesting of long-range plans; such pretesting can range from a formal decision laboratory to the exercise of executive judgment as specific phases of long-range planning are completed. The degree of refinement of the long-range testing procedures must depend on the knowledge available concerning the use of testing tools and the availability of funds to support the testing program.

8. Forecasting techniques should be developed to enable the company to prognosticate as accurately as possible the factors, forces, and effects which influence the environment in which the company will be competing. It should be remembered that forecasting is not planning; forecasting attempts to find the most probable course of events whereas planning should occur at a later date when the company evaluates the forecast information and from it develops objectives and plans for realizing the goals.

9. The management group should, in approaching the establishment of a long-range planning capability, endeavor to permeate the planning philosophy in the organizational structure so profoundly that planning becomes a function of all executives. The planning philosophy should extend beyond the frame of reference of the individuals and through the collective minds of the executive group rise above that group into the institutional mind of the corporation.

10. Insofar as possible alternative plans should be developed for the future to include not only diverse growth opportunities but also contraction of operations should economic conditions so dictate.

11. The results of long-range planning should be exploited to the fullest extent to include not only primary benefits such as new product development and reorganization but also ancillary advantages such as improved executive performance, improved communications, and providing a framework for operating decisions.

12. Specific recommendations relative to the requirement for future studies in long-range planning are suggested:

a. Much remains to be done to develop refined procedures and techniques for long-range planning in each company's functional area of effort.

b. A classical philosophical model should be developed which will provide a framework for the conduct of long-range planning in a business; such a philosophy should include the principal elements of long-range planning expressed in considerable detail; the absence of an integrated published study of long-range planning points out the need for such a model.

13. Finally it is recommended that all executive personnel realize
that any enduring organization has long-range as well as short-term responsibilities to its members, its customers, and to society in general;
consequently managers should develop the greatest possible capability
in shaping the future of their organization according to a carefully
selected image.

APPENDIX A

Tables portraying information gathering techniques used
in selecting companies to participate in the study.
Following tables cover industrials, life insurance companies, commercial banks, merchandising firms, transportation companies,
and utilities, in that order.

TABLE 51

TRANSPORTATION COMPANIES CONTACTED, RANKED BY OPERATING REVENUES
(1960)

Operating Revenues	No. of Companies in the U.S. (A)	% of Companies in the U.S. Col. (A) / 50 (B)	No. of Companies to be contacted: .30 x 50 x Col. (B) (C)
$400,000,000 and above	7	14.	2
$400,000,000 to 250,000,000	10	20.	3
$250,000,000 to 150,000,000	10	20.	3
$150,000,000 to 100,000,000	11	22.	3
$100,000,000 to 68,000,000	12	24.	4
Totals	50	100.	15

Note: Thirty per cent (15 companies) of the 50 largest Transportation Companies in the United States contacted.

TABLE 52

UTILITIES CONTACTED, RANKED BY ASSETS
(1960)

Assets	No. of Companies in the U.S. (A)	% of Companies in the U.S. Col. (A) / 50 (B)	No. of Companies to be contacted: .30 x 50 x Col. (B) (C)
$1,500,000,000 and above	7	14.	2
$1,500,000,000 to 1,000,000,000	8	16.	3
$1,000,000,000 to 600,000,000	17	34.	5
$600,000,000 to 475,000,000	7	14.	2
$475,000,000 to 380,000,000	11	22.	3
Totals	50	100.	15

Note: Thirty per cent (15 companies) of the 50 largest Utilities in the United States were contacted.

APPENDIX B

SAMPLE OF QUESTIONNAIRE MAILED TO CERTAIN LARGE AMERICAN BUSINESSES

Total responses to the questions are indicated on the questionnaire; however, narrative question response is not included because of the length and heterogeneity of such responses. In addition, certain questions that required a comprehensive quantitative response are not reflected in the completed questionnaire but are rather integrated appropriately in the text.

PREAMBLE

    Long-range planning is that activity whereby a systematic effort
to collect and analyze significant economic, technological, political,
social, and market data needed as a basis for forecasting events and conditions one or more years in the future is effected. This planning then
outlines how the company will acquire and use resources to achieve its
business goals and objectives in the forecast period.

    The following questionnaire is a combination "fill in", "check (✓)
off," and "narrative" answer type. In answering the questions requiring
a narrative response (in capital letters), please use additional sheets
if required. Some "check (✓) off" questions may require more than one
answer.

PLEASE MAIL COMPLETED QUESTIONNAIRE, ADDENDA, AND OTHER MATERIAL TO:

        Major David I. Cleland
        1320 Mapleridge Drive
        Fairborn, Ohio

LONG-RANGE PLANNING POLICY

1. Is your company now engaged in long-range planning? If answer is no, please answer questions 2 and 3 and return questionnaire. If answer is yes please fill out remainder of questionnaire and return.
   Yes (79)   No (7)

2. IF YOU DO NOT DO LONG-RANGE PLANNING, WHAT ARE YOUR REASONS FOR NOT DOING IT?   (See Text)

3. IF YOU DO NOT CONDUCT LONG-RANGE PLANNING AS SUCH, HOW DO YOU ANTICIPATE AND PREPARE FOR THE FUTURE OF YOUR COMPANY?   (See Text)

4. DOES YOUR LONG-RANGE PLANNING EFFORT COVER THE FORMULATION OF CONTRACTION OF OPERATIONS AS WELL AS EXPANSION PLANS?
   Contraction and Growth Plans (63)   Growth Plans Only (16)

5. Do your long-range planning techniques and philosophy contemplate the development of alternative long-range plans or just one best long-range plan?
   Alternative Plans (53)   One Best LRP (26)

6. Are your long-range planning activities done on a continuous or intermittent effort? (i.e., Do you have personnel working continuously (or just occasionally) on long-range planning?
   Continuous (56)   Intermittent (26)

DERIVATION OF LONG-RANGE PLANNING NEED

7. What year did you first begin effecting somewhat formal long-range planning activities within your company (or its ancestral company)?
   Year (   )   (See Text)

8. How did your company approach the task of getting middle and lower management support for the long-range planning activities?

Published suitable policy instruments	(33)
Formal instruction in long-range planning activities for executive personnel	(9)
Executive persuasion	(48)
Conducted seminars in long-range planning within the company	(25)

9. WHAT INTERNAL COMPANY CONDITIONS, IF ANY, NECESSITATED THE DEVELOPMENT OF A LONG-RANGE PLANNING ACTIVITY WITHIN YOUR COMPANY?
   (See Text)

10. WHAT EXTERNAL (NATIONAL, INDUSTRIAL, COMPETITIVE, INTERNATIONAL, ETC.) CIRCUMSTANCES MOTIVATED THE DEVELOPMENT OF A LONG-RANGE PLANNING ACTIVITY IN YOUR COMPANY?
    (See Text)

11. How did you go about setting up your long-range planning effort?
    Sought help from management consultant agencies   (22)
    Sought help from universities and colleges   (14)
    Sought help from government agencies   (6)
    Studied other companies' methods   (49)
    Studied current periodical and book literature   (49)
    Depended upon creative ability of company personnel   (73)

PLANNING PERIOD DETERMINANTS

12. What is your overall corporate long-range planning period?
    Over 1 year   (7)   Over 20 years   (3)
    Over 3 years   (14)   Over 30 years   (0)
    Over 5 years   (45)   Over 50 years   (2)
    Over 10 years   (21)

13. What factors determine how far ahead your company conducts long-range planning?
    Product development time   (43)
    Facilities construction time   (37)
    Raw materials availability   (12)
    Capital acquisition time   (21)
    Market development time   (58)
    Availability of accurate data   (31)
    Payoff time for capital investment (27)

14. Do you contemplate extending or contracting the period for which long-range plans are developed?
    Present period suitable   (59)
    Will extend   (15)
    Will contract   (0)
    Why are you changing the period for which long-range plans are developed?
    (If appropriate)   (See Text)

ORGANIZATION FOR LONG-RANGE PLANNING

15. When did you first establish a specific organizational entity for long-range planning responsibilities?   (   ) Year   (See Text)

16. Before you established an organizational entity for long-range planning, where was this function performed?
    By Board of Directors   (15)
    Pres. or Exec. Vice Pres.   (47)
    Other top officer personnel   (31)
    Additional duty of key officer   (11)
    Marketing/Sales Manager   (13)
    Financial Officer   (15)

17. What unique or specific organizational structure is used to accomplish long-range planning?

Long-range planning committee (21)
"Assistant to" for long-range planning (2)
Assigned as specific responsibility to a major functional area of effort (30)
Long-range planning office per se (27)

18. How many people are assigned full-time to the long-range planning function within your organization?

1-3 (21)   12-18 (3)
3-6 (14)   18-36 (5)
6-12 (9)   36-72 (2)

19. If you do not have anyone assigned full-time responsibilities for long-range planning, how many personnel spend a major part of their time in long-range planning activities? Number ( ) (See Text)

20. If you have a long-range planning staff, per se, what professional areas of effort are represented on this staff?

Economics (41)   Technical (42)
Statistics (33)   (Engineering)
Marketing (45)   Medical (1)
Management (41)   Personnel (8)
Finance (31)   Real Estate (4)
  (Including Accounting)
Production (21)
Legal (10)

21. If you do not have an economic staff as such, how do you obtain economic data for long-range planning?

Subscribe to outside economic advisory services (38)
Perusal by company executives of trade publications, newspapers, periodicals, govt. publications, etc. (35)
University contracts (7)
Hire economist on ad hoc basis (9)
Retain professional economist (10)
Part-time duty of specific company executive (19)
Attendance at professional meetings (24)
Provided by trade associations (26)
No special effort made to follow current economic conditions (2)

22. AT WHAT ORGANIZATIONAL LEVEL IS THE INDIVIDUAL IN CHARGE OF LONG-RANGE PLANNING ASSIGNED?   (See Text)

23. Have you ever used management consultants to do your long-range planning?   Yes (29)   No (48)

24. Do you now use management consultants to do your long-range planning?
      Yes (13)   No (66)

25. Do you use management consultants to furnish you with specific information necessary to your long-range planning?
Yes (42)   No (36)

26. How far down the organizational hierarchy do you require participation in long-range planning activities? (e.g., typical positions)
Through Executive Vice-President (16)
Through Vice-President for functional area of effort (29)
Through General Manager (32)
Through Superintendent (12)
Through General Foreman (4)
Through Department Chiefs (20)
Through Section Chiefs (13)

27. What sort of assistance and/or information do you seek from outside consultant agencies? Please double check (✓✓) type of assistance that is received most often.
Economic indicators (41)
Gross National Product Statistics (33)
Census of Manufacturers' Data (16)
Census of Business Data (20)
Economic Predictions (44)
Statistical Summaries (please specify) (17)
Legislative and technological evaluations (30)

28. IF YOU ARE USING A MANAGEMENT CONSULTANT FOR DOING YOUR LONG-RANGE PLANNING, WHAT ARE YOUR REASONS FOR THIS, RATHER THAN ACCOMPLISHING WORK USING COMPANY RESOURCES? (See Text)

29. WHAT, IF ANY, ARE YOUR OBJECTIONS TO USING A MANAGEMENT CONSULTANT TO DO ALL (OR A MAJOR PART) OF THE LONG-RANGE PLANNING WITHIN YOUR COMPANY? (See Text)

FUNCTIONAL AREAS OF LONG-RANGE PLANNING

30. Do you establish a master plan reflecting the long-range objectives of all major company functions for a prescribed period of future years?   Yes (46)   No (25)

31. Do you obtain assistance from trade associations in your long-range planning activities?   Yes (48)   No (26)
IF YES, WHAT TYPE OF ASSISTANCE?

32. IF YOU DO TRY TO EVALUATE THE LONG-RANGE PLANNING TECHNIQUES AND RESULTS OF YOUR INDUSTRY, HOW DO YOU DO THIS? (See Text)

33. Do you attempt to identify and integrate customer viewpoint, influences, and data into your long-range planning deliberations?
Yes (62)   No (6)
IF YES, BRIEFLY DESCRIBE THE MECHANICS OF HOW THIS IS ACCOMPLISHED.
(See Text)

34. This question pertains to the specific <u>functional</u> and <u>additional</u> areas examined in your long-range planning activities.

| Indicate in this column how far ahead you plan in the below areas. Express this period in terms of years, e.g., (2) | Check in this column the functional and additional areas you examine in your long-range planning activities. Please double check (✓✓) in this column the five (5) most critical areas of long-range planning in your company. |

(See Text)

( ) Product research and development	(48)	(44)
( ) Product costing	(25)	(10)
( ) Facilities	(50)	(38)
( ) Manufacturing/Production	(36)	(24)
( ) Finance	(50)	(36)
( ) Credit	(15)	(2)
( ) Marketing	(57)	(52)
( ) Organizational Structure	(32)	(9)
( ) Executive Development	(23)	(9)
( ) Industrial Relations	(17)	(6)
( ) Personnel	(31)	(17)
( ) Policy Formulation	(24)	(9)
( ) Public Relations	(15)	(1)
( ) Sources of Raw Materials	(21)	(11)
( ) Sources of Supplies	(17)	(2)
( ) Subcontracting	(14)	(1)
( ) Product Distribution	(26)	(6)
( ) Charity Contributions	(5)	(0)
( ) Product Engineering	(25)	(13)
( ) Real Estate	(17)	(7)
( ) Manufacturing Methods and Processes	(26)	(14)
( ) Product Competition	(38)	(21)
( ) Advertising	(14)	(3)
( ) "Size Planning," i.e., develop long-term objectives as to how large your business should be	(28)	(16)

35. What external factors are considered in your corporate long-range planning activities?

Legislative actions	(51)	Industry trends	(69)
Gross Natl. Product Changes	(47)	Competitors' actions	(67)
Government expenditures	(44)	International matters	(43)
Technological progress	(63)	Social mores	(10)
Population factors	(55)	Political environment	(36)
Business cycles	(49)	New construction	(29)
Fashion and styles	(7)	Employment	(23)
Housing statistics	(22)	Government fiscal policy	(43)
		Government controls	(46)

36. What key influences or factors <u>in your industry</u> do you evaluate?
        Competitive position   (73)
        Growth/decline trends   (74)
        Industry demands   (63)
        Individual firm's position   (66)
        Long-range planning techniques (35)

LONG-RANGE PLANNING PROCEDURES AND TECHNIQUES

37. What internal company data do you use in your long-range planning
    activities?
        Sales forecasts   (76)
        Present sales data   (71)
        Plant and equipment maturity data   (47)
        Credit data   (15)
        Financial data   (66)
        Cost data   (62)
        Personnel data   (50)
        Personnel capabilities   (46)
        Organization posture   (35)
        Manufacturing techniques   (50)
        Labor availability   (29)
        Product data   (55)

38. How do you pretest your long-range plans?
        Operations research   (18)   Ecological models   (1)
        Mathematical models   (15)   Coordination with manage-
        Executive seminars   (17)   ment consultant agencies (11)
        Computer techniques   (16)   No attempt to pretest   (3)
        "Business games"   (2)   Executive judgment   (63)
        Operational models   (10)

39. How frequently are your long-range plans reviewed?
        Quarterly   (8)   Every two years   (3)
        Semi-annually   (10)   Continuously   (30)
        Annually   (36)

40. HOW DO YOU DETERMINE THE TIME PERIOD FOR REVIEW?   (See Text)

41. WHAT SPECIAL LONG-RANGE PLANNING PROCEDURES HAVE BEEN ADOPTED FOR THE
    DECENTRALIZED UNITS WITHIN YOUR ORGANIZATION? (If such decentralized
    units exist)   (See Text)

42. What published source material do you use in effecting long-range
    planning?
        Government statistics   (75)   AMA Special Reports (44)
        Commerce Department Reports   (61)   University Business
        Trade Association Data   (60)   Research Reports (43)
        Books   (48)   Periodicals   (58)

43. What internal procedures and policies do you use for coordinating your long-range planning activities, e.g., in integrating your functional area long-range plans into a master long-range plan?

    Standing planning committee (25)
    Departmental seminar (13)
    Intracompany routing of master plan (14)
    Normal intrastaff coordination (49)
    Ad hoc "coordination" (28)
    Board of directors (15)

    NOTE: THIS IS BELIEVED TO BE AN EXCEEDINGLY IMPORTANT AREA OF EFFORT. PLEASE DESCRIBE FURTHER HOW YOU COORDINATE YOUR LONG-RANGE PLANNING ACTIVITIES. (See Text)

44. WHAT FUTURE MANAGERIAL INNOVATIONS DOES YOUR COMPANY PROPOSE TO DEVELOP AND IMPLEMENT IN ORDER TO IMPROVE AND REFINE PRESENT LONG-RANGE PLANNING TECHNIQUES? (See Text)

    No future refinements planned. (33)

LONG-RANGE PLANNING PROCESS

45. What forecasts do you attempt to make relative to your long-range planning activities?

    Sales (74)
    Technological progress (51)
    Political environment (29)
    International conditions (36)
    Legislative (24)
    Population trends (51)
    Gross National Product Changes (48)
    Government expenditures (45)
    Prices (53)
    Costs (55)
    Total customer potential (63)
    Standard of living progression (24)
    Capital availability (44)
    Profit (67)
    Marketing (36)
    Share of market (66)
    Product life (44)
    Product diversification (52)
    Employment requirements (38)
    Social mores (10)
    Consumer buying power (34)
    Industry trends (68)
    New construction (36)
    Raw material prices (30)

46. What tools do you use in long-range planning:
    Statistical analysis and inference   (66)
    Correlational and trend analysis   (59)
    Game theory   (9)
    Operations research   (29)
    Linear programming   (21)
    Break-even charts   (37)
    Budgets   (69)
    Financial statement   (65)
    Mathematical models   (20)
    Operational models   (11)
    Ecological models   (1)
    Input-output theory   (10)

47. Do you set long-range goals and/or objectives before you go into the long-range planning process or do the objectives grow out of the long-range planning processes?
    Establish objectives before entering into long-range
    planning   (29)
    Objectives grow out of preliminary long-range plan-
    ning activities   (57)
    Board of directors select long-term objectives upon
    which to predicate long-range planning   (6)
    Our long-term objectives can be established notwith-
    standing absence of long-range planning activities   (3)

48. After a long-range plan has been developed and accepted, how do you proceed to "communicate" it to those responsible for implementing it?
    Integrate into "master plan" and distribute to line
    managers   (12)
    Use company seminars   (14)
    Use intra-company briefings   (23)
    Distribute functional area long-range plans only;
    no attempt made to distribute "master plan"   (13)
    Integrate into "master plan" and distribute to all
    echelons responsible for implementing a portion
    of "master plan"   (12)
    Limited distribution of "master plan" as follows: (15)
    (See Text)
    No distribution effected. Line managers responsible
    for implementing own long-range plans and for com-
    pany coordination thereof   (4)

49. PLEASE EXPLAIN HOW YOU HAVE ATTEMPTED TO OVERCOME THE DIFFICULTIES LISTED IN QUESTION NO. 50.   (See Text)

50. This question treats with the difficulties and limitations, if any, that you have encountered in your long-range planning activities.

In this column please check the limitations and diffi-culties that you have had.

In this column please number (insofar as possible) the limitations and difficulties by order of importance, e.g., 1,2,3, etc. (See Text)

(45) Lack of accurate data ( )
(14) Gaining wholehearted top management support ( )
(28) Personnel limitations ( )
(46) Forecasting techniques ( )
(45) Preoccupation of management on immediate operating problems ( )
(35) Establishing long-range objectives ( )
(22) Establishing long-range planning policies, procedures, and techniques
(24) Having suitable organizational structure to effect long-range planning ( )
(29) Effecting intra-company coordination of long-range plan-ning activities ( )
(14) Business cycle influences ( )
(22) Government controls ( )
(20) Reviewing, revising and updating long-range plan ( )
(18) Industry peculiarities (Please explain)(See Text) ( )
(2) No difficulties or limitations

LONG-RANGE PLANNING RESULTS

51. Since World War II what organizational, product, or other changes have come about directly as a result of your long-range planning activities?
New product lines (39)
Organizational decentralization (18)
Company mergers (16)
Company acquisitions (36)
Executive development program (26)
Company reorganizations (26)
Product diversification (38)
No changes (13)

52. What "planning documents" are created within your company as a result of long-range planning?
"Master" plan for future (39)
Functional area long-range plans (37)
Long-range plan for specific segments of the company (45)
Economic predictions (36)

53. PLEASE SEND ME COPIES OF ANY COMPANY REGULATIONS, STANDARD OPERAT-
    ING PROCEDURES, LITERATURE, ORGANIZATIONAL CHARTS, POLICY INSTRU-
    MENTS AND SUCH RELATED PUBLICATIONS AS YOUR COMPANY USES DIRECTLY
    IN ITS LONG-RANGE PLANNING ACTIVITIES. PLEASE NOTE: I am not
    interested in company plans or specific techniques; rather what
    is desired is any unclassified corporate publications that exist
    for the guidance of the corporate long-range planning activities.
    (See Text)

54. PLEASE ADD ANY FURTHER INFORMATION YOU DESIRE ABOUT LONG-RANGE
    PLANNING.   (See Text)

55. Please check here if you desire a condensation of the study when
    it is completed. (65)

CORPORATIONS PARTICIPATING IN THE STUDY

Anheuser-Busch, Inc., St. Louis 18, Missouri

Aluminum Company of America, Pittsburgh 19, Pennsylvania

American President Lines, Ltd., San Francisco 4, California

American Bosch Arma Corporation, Hempstead, New York

Beech Aircraft Corporation, Wichita 1, Kansas

Bell & Howell Company, Chicago 45, Illinois

Bank of America National Trust & Savings Assn., San Francisco 20, Calif.

Bridgeport Brass Company, Bridgeport 2, Connecticut

Boeing Airplane Company, Seattle 24, Washington

Blaw-Knox Company, Pittsburgh 22, Pennsylvania

Clark Equipment Company, Buchanan, Michigan

Canada Dry Corporation, New York 17, New York

Curtis Publishing Company, Philadelphia 5, Penna.

Champion Paper & Fibre Company, Hamilton, Ohio

Chase Manhatten Bank, New York 5, New York

Caterpillar Tractor Company, Peoria 8, Illinois

Consolidated Electronics Industries Corporation, New York, New York

Colonial Stores, Inc., East Point, Georgia

Cessna Aircraft Company, Wichita 15, Kansas

Continental Can Company, Inc., New York 17, New York

Duquesne Light Company, Pittsburgh 19, Pennsylvania

E. I. duPont De Nemours & Co., Wilmington, Delaware

Fidelity Mutual Life Insurance Company, Philadelphia 1, Pennsylvania

First Western Bank & Trust Company, San Francisco 4, California

Food Machinery & Chemical Corporation, San Jose 10, California

Ford Motor Company, Dearborn, Michigan

First Pennsylvania Banking and Trust Company, Philadelphia 1, Penna.

Federal Paper Board Company, Inc., Bogota, New Jersey

General Tire and Rubber Company, Akron 9, Ohio

Grumman Aircraft Engineering Corporation, Bethpage, New York

Goodyear Aircraft Corporation, Akron, Ohio

General Foods Corporation, White Plains, New York

General Mills, Inc., Minneapolis 26, Minn.

General Electric Company, Schenectedy 5, New York

Hart, Schaffner & Marx, Chicago 6, Illinois

Hiller Aircraft Corporation, Palo Alto, California

Hercules Powder Company, Wilmington 99, Delaware

International Shoe Company, St. Louis 66, Missouri

International Business Machines Corporation, New York 22, New York

Kaiser Aluminum & Chemical, Oakland 12, California

Kelsey-Hayes, Detroit, Michigan

Kimberly-Clark Corporation, Neenah, Wisconsin

Koppers Company, Inc., Pittsburgh 19, Pennsylvania

Kern County Land Company, San Francisco 8, California

Ling-Temco (Vought) Electronics, Dallas 22, Texas

Lear, Inc., Santa Monica, California

Mellon National Bank & Trust Company, Pittsburgh 30, Pennsylvania

Mead Corporation, Chillicothe, Ohio

Minneapolis-Honeywell Regulator Company, Minneapolis 8, Minnesota

Minnesota Mining & Mfg. Co., St. Paul 6, Minnesota

McDonnell Aircraft Corp., St. Louis 3, Missouri

McGraw-Hill Publishing Co., New York 36, New York

Metropolitan Life Insurance Co., New York 10, New York

National Cash Register Company, Dayton, Ohio

National Biscuit Company, New York 22, New York

Northrop Corporation, Beverly Hills, California

North American Aviation, Inc., Los Angeles 45, California

Provident Mutual Life Insurance Co. of Philadelphia, Philadelphia 39, Pa.

Pittsburgh National Bank, Pittsburgh 30, Pennsylvania

Pennsylvania Power and Light Company, Allentown, Pennsylvania

Pacific Gas and Electric Company, San Francisco 6, California

Phillips Petroleum Company, Bartlesville, Oklahoma

Peoples Gas Light & Coke Company, Chicago 3, Illinois

Pet Milk Company, St. Louis 1, Missouri

Pittsburgh Steel Company, Pittsburgh 19, Pennsylvania

Rohr Aircraft Corporation, Chula Vista, California

Royal-McBee Corporation, New York 22, New York

Republic Aviation Corporation, Farmingdale, Long Island, New York

R. J. Reynolds Tobacco Company, Winston-Salem, North Carolina

Red Owl Stores, Incorporated, Minneapolis 1, Minnesota

Rexall Drug & Chemical Company, Los Angeles 54, California

Southland Life Insurance Company, Dallas 1, Texas

Spiegel, Incorporated, Chicago 9, Illinois

Southern California Edison Company, Los Angeles 53, California

Sun Oil Company, Philadelphia 3, Pennsylvania

Thompson Ramo Wooldridge Incorporated, Cleveland 17, Ohio

Technical Services, Incorporated, Dallas, Texas

Travelers Insurance Company, Hartford 15, Connecticut

Time, Incorporated, New York 20, New York

Texas Instruments, Incorporated, Dallas 9, Texas

Thiokol Chemical Corporation, Bristol, Pennsylvania

United Aircraft Corporation, East Hartford 8, Connecticut

United States Lines Company, New York 4, New York

Union Bag-Camp Paper Corporation, New York 7, New York

United Air Lines, Incorporated, Chicago 38, Illinois

Whirlpool Corporation, St. Joseph, Michigan

Westinghouse Electric Corporation, Pittsburgh 30, Pennsylvania

Western Electric Company, New York 7, New York

Wyandotte Chemicals Corporation, Wyandotte, Michigan

Weyerhaeser Company, Tacoma 1, Washington

BIBLIOGRAPHY

A. BOOKS

Bloom, Gordon F. and Herbert R. Rorthrup. Economics of Labor Relations. Homewood, Illinois: Richard D. Irwin, Inc., 1961.

Brown, Alvin. Organization, A Formulation of Principle. New York: Hibbert Printing Company, 1945.

_____. Organization of Industry. New York: Prentice-Hall, Inc., 1947. 205-206.

Bursk, Edward C. and Dan H. Fenn, Jr. (eds.). Planning The Future Strategy Of Your Business. New York: McGraw-Hill Book Company, Inc., 1956.

Chase, Stuart & Others. The Social Responsibility of Management. New York: School of Commerce, Accounts, and Finance, New York University, 1950.

Clark, John M. Social Control of Business. New York: McGraw-Hill Book Company, Inc., 1939.

Clausewitz, Karl von. On War. Translated from the German by O. J. Matthijis Jolles. Washington, D.C.: Infantry Journal Press, 1943.

Dale, Ernest and Lyndall F. Urwick. Staff In Organization. New York: McGraw-Hill Book Company, Inc., 1960.

Davis, Ralph Currier. The Fundamentals of Top Management. New York: Harper & Brothers, Publishers, 1951.

Dennison, Henry. Organization Engineering. New York: McGraw-Hill Book Co., Inc., 1931.

Dimock, Marshall E. A Philosophy of Administration Toward Creative Growth. New York: Harper & Brothers, Publishers, 1958.

Drury, Horace B. Scientific Management: A History and Criticism. New York: Columbia University Press, 1915.

Ewing, David W. (ed.). Long-Range Planning For Management. New York: Harper & Brothers, Publishers, 1958.

Fayol, Henri. General and Industrial Management. London: Pitman, 1949.

Fenn, Dan H. Management In A Rapidly Changing Economy. New York: McGraw-Hill, 1958.

Gantt, H. L. Organizing For Work. New York: Harcourt, Brace & Howe, 1919.

279

Gibson, Weldon B. "Guideposts For Forward Planning," Long-Range Planning For Management. Edited by David W. Ewing. New York: Harper & Brothers, 1958.

Gilbreth, Frank B. Science In Management For The One Best Way To Do Work. Milan: Societa Umanitaria, 1922.

Goerlitz, Walter. History of The German General Staff. New York: Praeger, Inc., 1953.

Hempel, Edward H. Top-Management Planning; Methods Needed For Post-War Orientation of Industrial Companies. New York: Harper & Brothers, 1945.

Hittle, J. D. The Military Staff, Its History and Development. Harrisburg: The Military Service Publishing Co., 1949.

Holden, Paul E., Launsbury S. Fish, and Hubert L. Smith. Top Management Organization and Control. Stanford University, California: Stanford University Press, 1946.

Keynes, John Maynard. The General Theory of Employment, Interest, and Money. London: Harcourt, Brace and Company, Inc., 1936.

Koontz, Harold and Cyril O'Donnell. Principles of Management. New York: McGraw-Hill Book Company, Inc., 1959.

Larson, Henrietta M. Guide To Business History. Cambridge: Harvard University Press, 1948.

LeBreton, Preston P. and Dale A. Henning. Planning Theory. Englewood Cliffs, New Jersey: Prentice-Hall, Inc., 1961.

Lepawsky, Albert. Administration; The Art and Science of Organization and Management. New York: A. A. Knopf, 1949.

Marshall, Alfred. Principles of Economics. Eighth Edition. MacMillan & Co., Ltd.

Mee, John Franklin. A History of Twentieth Century Management Thought. The Ohio State University, 1959 Doctoral Dissertation.

Metcalf, Henry C. The Psychological Foundations of Management. New York: A. W. Shaw Company, 1927.

Mooney, James D. The Principles of Organization. New York: Harper, 1947.

Neilson, William Allan, (ed.). Webster's New International Dictionary of The English Language. Second Edition, Unabridged. Springfield, Mass.: G. & C. Merriam Company, Publishers, 1960.

Nelson, Major General Otto L., Jr. National Security and The General Staff. Washington: Infantry Journal, 1946.

NewBury, Frank D. Business Forecasting; Principles and Practice. New York: McGraw-Hill, 1952.

Newman, William H. Administrative Action. New York: Prentice-Hall, Inc., 1951.

Poor's Register of Directors and Executives. New York: Standard & Poor's Corporation, 1961.

Roosevelt, Franklin D. Looking Forward. The John Day Company, 1933.

Robinson, Webster. Fundamentals of Business Organization. New York: McGraw-Hill Book Co., 1925.

Sheldon, Oliver. The Philosophy of Management. London: Sir Isaac Pitman & Sons, Ltd., 1923.

The Oxford English Dictionary. Vol. VII. N-Poy. Oxford: The Clarendon Press, 1933.

B. PERIODICALS

Beishline, J. R. "Influence of Military Management," Advanced Management (August, 1955), 11.

Bishop, Warren. "Rain of Plans," Nation's Business (August, 1931).

Bleiberg, R. M. "Industry's Planners--Better Than Governments," Barrons (November, 1946), 3.

Brown, Donaldson. "Forecasting and Planning Vital To Industrial Prosperity: Method of General Motors Corporation," Iron Age (May, 1928), 1321-1322.

_____. "Forecasting and Planning as a Factor in Stabilizing Industry," Sales Management (January-February, 1929), 258-259.

Cassels, Louis and Raymond L. Randall. "Long-Range Planning," Nation's Business (August, 1961), 83.

Cresap, Mark W., Jr. "Some Guides To Long-Term Planning," N.A.C.A. Bulletin (January, 1958), 602.

Davis, R. C. "What The Staff Function Actually Is," Advanced Management (May, 1954), 16.

Donald, W. J. "Forget Your Jitters--And Have A Plan," Forbes (March, 1933), 8.

Drucker, Peter F. "Long-Range Planning, Challenge To Management Science," Management Science (April, 1949), 238.

_____. "Thinking Ahead," Harvard Business Review (January, 1959), Vol. 37, p. 146.

Eide, R. "Planning Ahead--The Place of Commercial Research," Special Libraries (July, 1931), 240-246.

Ewing, David W. "Looking Around: Long-Range Business Planning," Harvard Business Review (July-August, 1956), 135-146.

Feiker, F. M. "Sensible Economic Planning," Printers Ink (March, 1932), 71-72.

Foulice, R. A. "Prepare Your Business For Tomorrow," Duns Review (April, 1937), 47-48.

Fisch, Gerald F. and Dean L. Jacoby. "Long-Range Planning--An Approach To Leadership," Cost and Management (April, 1959), 147.

Frame, S. T. "Planning For The Future Of News Print," Paper Trade Journal (April, 1932), 18.

Gustin, R. P. and S. A. Holme. "Approach To Post War Planning," Harvard Business Review (July, 1942), 459-472.

Hall, S. P. "Eyes on the Next Decade: A Forward Planning Procedure," NACA Bulletin (December, 1948), 375-380.

Harvar, J. G. "The American General Staff," The Saturday Evening Post (March, 1936), 51.

Heermance, E. L. "Trade Association's Part in Coordinate Planning," Mechanical Engineering (February, 1933), 103.

Hill, William E. and Charles H. Granger. "Charting Your Company's Future Growth," Dun's Review and Modern Industry (August, 1957), 43.

"Industry Plans For The Future," Conference Board Business Record Vol. 9, (August, 1952), 324-328.

Kettering, D. F. "Today's Need--More Planning and Less Executing," Iron Age (May, 1933), 733.

Miller, E. "Long-Range Planning: Overview," Advanced Management (November, 1960), 8-11.

Neuhoff, Malcolm C. and G. Clark Thompson. "Industry Plans For The Future," Business Record (August, 1952), 326.

Payne, Bruce. "Steps in Long-Range Planning," Harvard Business Review (March-April, 1957), 95-106.

Person, H. S. "On Planning," The Society For The Advancement of Management Journal (December, 1936), 143.

_____. "On the Technique of Planning," Bulletin of the Taylor Society and of The Society of Industrial Engineers (November, 1934), 29.

Platt, William J. & N. Robert Maines. "Pretest Your Long-Range Plans," Harvard Business Review (January-February, 1959), 119-127.

Pinchbeck, R. B. "Planning Is a Big Problem of Business," Domestic Engineering (September, 1931), 91.

Prentis, H. W., Jr. "Liberal Education For Business and Industry," Bulletin of The American Association of University Professors (Autumn, 1952), 346.

Purkey, L. L. "Organization Planning: A Continuing Job; Standard Oil Company of California; Abstract," Management Review (April, 1944), 117-118.

Quinn, James Brian. "Long-Range Planning of Industrial Research," Harvard Business Review (July-August, 1961).

Schell, E. H. "Training Men To Look Ahead," Nation's Business (March, 1940), 30.

_____. "Long-Term Company Planning; New Importance to Business," Dun's Review (January, 1943), 19.

Steiner, George A. "What Do We Know About Using Long-Range Plans," California Management Review (Fall, 1959), 93.

Taylor, Frederick W. "A Piece-Rate System," Transactions (American Society of Mechanical Engineers), XVI (1895), 856-58.

Tulley, Shelley, Jr., and Andrall W. Pearson. "A Blue-Print For Long-Range Planning," Business Horizons (1961).

Whitmore, E. "Organization Plan For Expansion: Johns-Manville Reorganizes Executive Duties," American Business (November, 1946), 56-57.

Wrapp, H. Edward. "Organization For Long-Range Planning," Harvard Business Review (January-February, 1957), 37-47.

"Broad Aspects of Industrial Planning Discussed by Taylor Society," Iron Age (May, 1931), 1534.

"Building For Growth," Electrical World (May, 1937), 79-84.

"Business Probes Its Own Structure; Review of Planning and Developing the Company Organization Structure," Business Week (September 20, 1952), 84-91.

"Day to Day vs Long Pull Planning For Business Profits," American Business Combined With System (November, 1938), 25.

"The Fortune Directory," Fortune (July, 1961), 167-186; "The Fortune Directory," Fortune (Part II, August, 1961), 129-138.

"Planning Business Stability," Nation's Business (November, 1931), 56-58.

"Plan Tomorrow's Profits," Nation's Business (August, 1958), 76.

"Why Companies Grow," Nation's Business (November, 1957), 2.

C. NEWSPAPERS

The Wall Street Journal, October 25, 1961.

D. PUBLICATIONS OF GOVERNMENT

Twelfth Census of The United States, Vol. VII, Chapter 2.

E. SPEECHES

Schriever, Bernard A., General, Commander, Air Force Systems Command, "The Real Challenge To Military Management," as reported in Armed Forces Management (February, 1962), 40.

Cordiner, Ralph J. Speech to the Economic Club of New York, as reported in The Harbus News (December 21, 1956).

F. LETTERS

Letter, Continental Can Company, Inc., dated February 27, 1962.

G. UNPUBLISHED MATERIALS

<u>The Corporate Planner and His Job.</u> (Report No. 125) Menlo Park, Calif.:
Stanford Research Institute.

Maines, N. R. <u>Why Companies Grow.</u> Menlo Park, Calif.: Stanford Research
Institute, 1957.

AUTOBIOGRAPHY

I, David Ira Cleland, was born in Portersville, Pennsylvania, March 21, 1926. I received my secondary-school education in the public schools of Butler County, Pennsylvania, and at the Kiski Prep School, Saltsburg, Pennsylvania. My undergraduate training was taken at the University of Pittsburgh, which granted me the Bachelor of Arts degree in 1954. From the University of Pittsburgh I also received the Master of Business Administration degree in 1958. In September, 1960, I entered the Ohio State University for the Doctor of Philosophy residency and was admitted to candidacy in August, 1961.

I have served over fifteen years of active federal service in the Armed Forces of the United States, five of which were served in foreign lands. I presently hold a Major's commission in the Regular Air Force of the United States and now serve as a Production and Procurement Staff Officer in the C/KC 135 Project Office, Wright-Patterson Air Force Base, Dayton, Ohio.